At Issue

| Food Security

Other Books in the At Issue Series

At Issue

| Food Security

Kathryn Roberts, Book Editor

GREENHAVEN
PUBLISHING

Published in 2021 by Greenhaven Publishing, LLC
353 3rd Avenue, Suite 255, New York, NY 10010

Articles in Greenhaven Publishing anthologies are often edited for length to meet page
requirements. In addition, original titles of these works are changed to clearly present
the main thesis and to explicitly indicate the author's opinion. Every effort is made to
ensure that Greenhaven Publishing accurately reflects the original intent of the authors.
Every effort has been made to trace the owners of the copyrighted material.

Cover image: Gajus/Shutterstock.com

Library of Congress Cataloging-in-Publication Data

Names: Roberts, Kathryn, 1990– editor.
Title: Food security / Kathryn Roberts, book editor.
Description: New York : Greenhaven Publishing, 2021. | Series: At issue |
    Includes bibliographical references and index. | Audience: Grades 9–12.
Identifiers: LCCN 2020000162 | ISBN 9781534507364 (library binding) | ISBN
    9781534507357 (paperback)
Subjects: LCSH: Food supply—Juvenile literature. | Food security—Juvenile
    literature. | Food—Safety measures—Juvenile literature.
Classification: LCC HD9000.5 .F596426 2020 | DDC 338.1/9—dc23
LC record available at https://lccn.loc.gov/2020000162

Manufactured in the United States of America

Website: http://greenhavenpublishing.com

Contents

Introduction

I s there enough food to feed the world? The answer may surprise you, but it's actually yes. Despite the fact that there are many parts of the world that struggle to produce enough fresh food—including in our own backyard—there is actually enough out there that world hunger should not exist.[1]

But despite this fact, it does exist. According to a study by McGill University and the University of Minnesota, the world already produces more than one and a half times enough food to feed everyone on the planet—enough to feed 10 billion people.[2] That global food production rate has increased faster than the rate of population growth, and doesn't look to be slowing down, especially with the advent of new technology in the farming sector.

The current world population, as of 2019, is 7.7 billion people, which is well below the 10 billion people that global food production can support.[3] But with an ever-increasing life expectancy, we're going to see more people living longer, and we are also going to see more people living hungrier.

This is because the problem is not that there is a lack of food to go around—far from it. No matter how it may seem, the facts are the facts, and there is enough food to go around. Instead, hunger is caused by systemic poverty and inequality combined with climate change, economic instability, and war.

Organizations around the world are working to solve the tricky problem that is world hunger, from the United Nations to Mercy Corps, but it's far from easy. This is because hunger is so intimately connected to other major international issues like climate change, poverty, and the growing international refugee crisis.

Of course, it's not enough to just feed a person and claim that world hunger has been solved. The issue of world hunger is centered on how to make it possible to feed someone healthily.

The healthier a person is—especially a child—the healthier the population as a whole.

Unfortunately, the cycle of hunger is systemically engrained in many parts of the world, and it all too often starts from childhood. When a family must prioritize how much they can afford to spend on food, they're likely to decide to spend more on continuing to keep a roof over their heads rather than healthier but pricier food options. And when an emergency strikes? People will often skip meals in order to cope with that financial burden.

Studies have also shown that poor nutrition leads to poor health, and it is very expensive to be sick, both in the United States and in many other countries that choose not to guarantee healthcare to all citizens. For a child who grows up hungry, the chronic health issues that they develop can potentially keep them out of school. That lack of education limits their ability to find work that pays a living wage, and the cycle of poverty and undernourishment continues into the next generation.

Another issue that makes a serious impact on world hunger is food waste. So much of the world's food—more than one-third of all food produced, according to the Food and Agricultural Organization of the United Nations (FAO)—does not end up in the hands of those who need it.[4] Rather, it ends up in landfills. This is sometimes due to practices that don't allow food to be donated, but also due to poor storage facilities that allow food to rot before it even has the chance to be sold.

The biggest food-wasting culprits are Europe and North America, where 209 pounds of food per capita is thrown away each year.[5] This is compared to places in South and Southeastern Asia and sub-Saharan Africa, which only throw away about thirteen to twenty-four pounds of food each year. In the United States, food accounts for 21 percent of the solid waste in American landfills.[6] Fortunately, there is an economic benefit toward reducing food waste in America. It can potentially generate an economic value of $10 billion for both companies and consumers, reduce water demand by 1.6 trillion gallons, and maybe even create

15,000 new jobs, which would allow people to move out of the cycle of hunger that they have been trapped in due to the issue of food waste.[7]

But perhaps the biggest issue impacting world hunger is war. Afghanistan, a country of 31 million, tops the international list of countries unable to produce enough food to feed its population.[8] The county has one of the world's largest populations of internally displaced people due to violence and natural disasters. More than half of the internally displaced people in Afghanistan, including farmers, don't have enough food to feed their families. One significant reason is the existence of the militant Taliban organization, which denies Afghan citizens the stability needed to grow their own food.

Sudan has also been a victim of violence, with two civil wars causing 41,000 people to be displaced as a consequence of conflict and violence.[9] Furthermore, Sudan has received an influx of more than 2.4 million refugees from South Sudan, who also require food assistance. What Afghanistan and Sudan also have in common, along with their history of food access being impeded by war, is food access being disrupted by climate disasters—specifically drought and flooding. In the Sudan, more than 121,000 people were displaced in 2018 due to natural disasters, along with the displacement caused by war.

Per the Global Hunger Index, the continent of Africa is the hungriest in the world, with the Central African Republic topping the list of hungriest countries in the world in 2019.[10] The country has been a victim of both political instability and ethnic violence, which has disrupted food production and supply to a population of about 5 million. Numerous African countries have been hit with both war and climate disaster, making the area increasingly dependent on outside aid to feed its people. In fact, it is estimated by the Potsdam Institute that by 2050, more than half of the world's population will have to rely on food sourced from other countries. However, even some of the wealthiest countries in the world—the

United States, China, Germany, Japan, and the United Kingdom—import billions of dollars in food each year.[11]

Though hunger is a global crisis, it's also important to remember that food instability and insecurity exist in our own backyard. In the 27,000-square mile reservation the Navajo Nation calls home—which extends into Utah, Arizona, and New Mexico—fresh food is both scarce and expensive. But it's not just areas that are typically seen as disenfranchised that are considered food deserts in the United States. Major metropolitan areas are also considered food deserts, including neighborhoods in cities like San Francisco, New Orleans, Chicago, and New York City.

The viewpoints featured in *At Issue: Food Security* take into consideration not just the overall impact of food insecurity around the world and who is impacted the most, but also what can be done to mitigate these issues locally. Through greater understanding of the many factors that cause hunger, perhaps it may be possible to decrease it going forward.

Notes

1. Eric Holt-Gimenez, "We Already Grow Enough Food for 10 Billion People—and Still Can't End Hunger," *HuffPost*, May 2, 2012.

2. Verena Seufert, Navin Ramankutty, and Jonathan A. Foley, "Comparing the yields of organic and conventional agriculture," *Nature*, April 25, 2012.

3. "World Population Prospects 2019," United Nations Department of Economic and Social Affairs, 2019.

4. "Food Loss and Food Waste," Food and Agriculture Organization of the United Nations," December 13, 2019.

5. Valerie Jaffee, "Americans Throw Away Their Weight in Food Every Year," Greenbiz, May 13, 2011.

6. "International Efforts on Wasted Food Recovery, EPA, May 6, 2019.

7. *Ibid.*

8. Lanessa Cago, "Countries Most Dependent on Others for Food," World Atlas, December 5, 2017.

9. Carolyn Kenney, "How Climate Change and Water and Food Insecurity Drive Instability," Center for American Progress, November 30, 2017.

10. "2019 Global Hunger Index by Severity," Global Hunger Index, 2019.

11. Lanessa Cago, "Countries Most Dependent on Others for Food," World Atlas, December 5, 2017.

1

What Is Food Security?

Mercy Corps

Mercy Corps is a global team of humanitarians who partner with communities, corporations, and governments to transform lives around the world.

In the following viewpoint, Mercy Corps details its approach toward improving the lives of more than 14.5 million people in more than forty countries. One out of seven people are at risk of malnutrition, making it one of the deadliest and most widespread health issues facing the world. The viewpoint goes on to detail the four variables that define what it means to be "food secure," including availability, access, utilization, and risk management.

M ercy Corps helps people in the world's toughest places turn the crises of natural disaster, poverty and conflict into opportunities for progress. Driven by local needs and market conditions, our programs provide communities with the tools and support they need to transform their own lives. Our worldwide team of 3,700 professionals is improving the lives of 14.5 million people in more than 40 countries. In recognition that access to adequate food and nutritional sustenance is integral to the success of relief and development programming, Mercy Corps currently operates upwards of 40 food security development projects in over 20 countries, worth approximately $200 million. These projects

"Food Security: Sector Approach 2009," by Mercy Corps, www.mercycorps.org/research/food-security. Reprinted by permission.

work with communities and households to develop and implement sustainable approaches to meeting their own food needs and improve food availability, access and utilization, as well as the ability to withstand shocks.

It is estimated that more than 1 billion people live in hunger.[1] That means one person in every seven is at risk from one of the most deadly and widespread health issues in the world today, malnutrition. UNICEF estimates 60 percent of child deaths in developing countries are from malnutrition, and those that survive hunger in the early stages of life are at risk from irreparable physical and mental health issues. While this level of health and hunger is severe, the food security sector offers an effective leverage point to alleviate this suffering: The UN claims there is enough food on the planet to provide the global population with a healthy and nutritious diet. Agriculture plays a crucial role in developing countries where the 450 million small farms—two hectares or less—are home to about 2 billion people, comprising roughly 46 percent of the global workforce.[2] Improvements in health care, water and sanitation conditions and hygienic household practices can allow children to grow up well nourished and families to maintain good health and nutrition status. Mercy Corps believes that the human capital exists to eradicate chronic hunger and malnutrition. Our food security programs attempt to catalyze this potential in order to find viable long-term solutions to the availability, access and utilization of food resources.

The design and implementation of our food security programming is proving to be effective for the complex, transitional environments in which we work. Our field reports show there is clear synergy with our agricultural, economic development and health sectors, as well as the Mercy Corps Action Center to End World Hunger and our environmental and conflict management programming.

What Is Food Security?

Defining Food Security

Food security is commonly defined as "when all people, at all times, have physical, social and economic access to sufficient, safe and nutritious food which meets their dietary needs and food preferences for an active and healthy life."[3] Four interrelated variables are central to achieving food security:

1. Food Availability—when sufficient quantity is consistently available to all individuals through household production, domestic output, commercial imports or food assistance.

2. Food Access—when households and all individuals have adequate resources to obtain appropriate foods for a nutritious diet. Access depends on income available to the household, distribution of food among members of the household and the price of food.

3. Food Utilization—the proper use of food requires a diet with sufficient energy and essential nutrients, potable water and adequate sanitation. Effective utilization depends on good health and knowledge within households of basic principals of nutrition and proper childcare.

4. Risk Management—the degree to which individuals, households or communities can cope with and withstand stressful situations and shocks. Vulnerability can be grouped into five categories by risk factors: environmental, market, political, social and health. Inability to manage risks can lead to food insecurity.

Food Secure Households

A food secure household is one that can produce, or access, sufficient amounts of nutritious food for all family members, one that enjoys good health and sanitation facilities and practices, and one that is resilient to shocks that might make the household vulnerable again. In other words, a food secure household has met its essential health, economic and productive needs. While the household might still be poor, its members are not challenged by day-to-day threats to its survival caused by lack of food, and can work towards longer-term development priorities.

Mercy Corps' Food Security Approach

Food Security Sector Mission

Through its food security programming, Mercy Corps aims to empower households and communities to develop and implement sustainable approaches to meeting their own food needs and improve food availability, access and utilization, as well as the ability to withstand shocks.

Food Availability

The first necessary condition for food security is straightforward: food must be available to be consumed. Mercy Corps approaches issues of availability through several means, including building agricultural production, improving access to markets and providing food distribution. Mercy Corps works with small farmers to increase agricultural production, through providing inputs or capacity building, in order to increase household consumption, as well as a source of income. Mercy Corps' emergency and developmental relief programs work in situations in which there has been a food deficit and food distribution has been urgently needed to provide vulnerable people with sufficient caloric intake.

Our agricultural development initiatives play a pivotal roll in facilitating food security for the people we serve. This sector takes a market driven approach to ensure scaled and sustainable impact results. Mercy Corps maps out the interrelationships between buyers, sellers, producers and end consumers along respective value chains and intervenes through a variety of means such as infrastructure improvements, technical assistance, financing and technology upgrades. Programs create and support agricultural market systems that favor economic growth for the largest number of smallholder farmers and related agri-business entrepreneurs.

The outcome of this includes the greater availability of nutritious and affordable food in local consumer markets.

Food Access

While food may be available, there is no guarantee that all household members will be able to access it. Lack of purchasing power keeps many families from obtaining the food necessary for a healthy and productive life. Mercy Corps works at a grassroots level to help households sustainably build their income. While we work on economic development on many levels, food security programming focuses on the most vulnerable.

Mercy Corps' market development programming plays a vital role in increasing incomes and productivity in market systems, ultimately facilitating access to food resources. The sector takes a progressive approach that leads communities and entrepreneurs from relief to sustainable livelihoods to long-term economic growth. Every context is different, and programming builds on the unique economic potential of each country. Engaging with entrepreneurs and producers at the community level as well as with lead firms and buyers, Mercy Corps helps ensure poor families and vulnerable communities benefit from the increased revenues that result from market improvements and sector growth. As economies grow, so does the access to available food and the nutritional health of the households and communities we serve.

Food Utilization

Being able to produce or purchase food is not sufficient to ensure a healthy life: food needs to be selected and prepared appropriately, with adequate health care, child care and water and sanitation conditions in place. Mercy Corps addresses underlying causes of food insecurity through programs that address maternal and child health issues, safe water provision, hygiene and sanitation practices and HIV/AIDS education, prevention and rehabilitation. This permits the body to effectively utilize the food it consumes.

Mercy Corps' programs tackle critical health issues and disparities through community-based activities carried out alongside public and private partners, focusing on maternal and child health, community nutrition, fighting infectious diseases and improving water and sanitation. Receiving sufficient calories and micronutrients from the womb through the age of 24 months is essential for a child to reach his or her physical and cognitive potential, and avoid the lifelong condition of stunting. Mercy Corps promotes sound practices in pre- and post-natal care, breastfeeding, introduction of complementary feeding and proper child care so that caregivers can achieve and maintain good health for their children. As diseases such as HIV/AIDS greatly compromise people's health and food security, Mercy Corps implements programs to prevent further infection and to protect the livelihoods of those living with the disease. We also work to improve water and sanitation conditions and hygiene practices, understanding the intimate connection between sound hygiene and sustainable health and nutrition status.

Risk Management—Establishing Resiliency

If the components of availability, access and utilization cannot be sustained, then households cannot realistically be considered as food secure. Mercy Corps' programs work towards long-term solutions to food insecurity through a variety of approaches. At the time that food security programs are designed, Mercy Corps seeks to identify the longer-term causes of insecurity, be they social, political, environmental, health or market related. Program activities directly address those threats, and promote systems and structures that will enable food security sustainability. Such systems can also provide platforms for ongoing community development.

Mercy Corps' climate and environment sector is helping to address one of the greatest risks to long-term food security: climate change. Recognizing that climate change threatens to undermine any development or food security progress made to date in support of the populations that we serve, Mercy Corps implements a variety of program interventions aimed at both mitigating and adapting to the impacts of this worldwide phenomenon. Through the means of alternative energy, sustainable resource management and advocacy and outreach, Mercy Corps is helping communities fortify gains made to their food security for the foreseeable future.

Using Food Resources

Mercy Corps implements several programs that use food resources to address food insecurity. These resources are utilized in the following ways:

- **Distribution**—Food is provided directly to beneficiaries. The goals of distribution include recuperation (providing nutritional and caloric intake to the malnourished to allow them to attain good health), prevention (providing food resources so that malnutrition does not occur) and incentive (motivating beneficiaries to participate in program activities, such as Food for Work or health education). An advantage of distribution programs is that they can be an excellent way of targeting the most vulnerable: food resources must be of value to participants in relation to their own time and effort, so self-selection of the very poor occurs. A disadvantage is the potential for creating dependency, and the increased difficulty of exit strategies: transitioning to other kinds of development may seem more abrupt when one element of that transition is the discontinuation of food rations. Mercy Corps addresses this by making sure that other activities address the root causes of food insecurity so that a household will be more self-sufficient by the time food distributions cease.
- **Barter**—Commodities are shipped to beneficiary country and processed (for example, enriched flour into biscuits). The processed product is then either distributed or monetized in pursuit of program objectives. Barter provides a means for supporting processing industries and producing culturally and nutritionally appropriate products.
- **Monetization**—Commodities are shipped to beneficiary country and sold (usually in bulk) on the market; income

is used to fund program activities. If commodities are chosen correctly, they match unsatisfied demand in the recipient country, so that both commodity sale and subsequent program meet local needs. Most programs funded by monetization are required to specifically address food security issues. In particular, the US Department of Agriculture (a frequent donor for monetization programs) targets agricultural development and agricultural markets.

All Mercy Corps programs using food resources start with an analysis of the market impact of bringing commodities into the country (for US government-funded programs, this is known as the Bellmon Analysis). For example, will the import of such commodities negatively impact agricultural production or the business of local traders? Food resources should only be brought into a country if demand outstrips supply and analysis finds no significant risk of negative consequences.

Notes

1 UN WFP, http://www.wfp.org/hunger/stats

2 World Bank Development Database.

3 USAID key concepts, adopted at World Food Summit of 1996, reconfirmed at World Food Summit of 2002.

2

Achieving a World with Zero Hunger

Linda Qian

Linda Qian is a post-graduate research fellow at the Asia Pacific Foundation of Canada, Canada's leading organization for research, analysis, and consultation on Canada-Asia relations.

In an effort to bring about a world with zero hunger, this viewpoint details how China has been able to bring down its percentage of the population that is undernourished from 24.5 percent in 1991 to 9.2 percent at the time this viewpoint was published in 2016. Considering the issue of the air quality in China, there are concerns about food grown in Chinese soil being contaminated as a result. Through collaboration with other countries, including Canada, China has been able to make strides by providing a crop that is heartier and more environmentally friendly.

According to figures provided by the UN's Food and Agriculture Organization (FAO), 9.2% of China's population is undernourished. Although China has made tremendous strides in bringing this figure down from the staggering 24.5% in 1991, this still means that 133.8 million people in China remain undernourished. This is not just an issue of spreading adequate quantities of food across the population; food quality has also been flagged as a high priority concern by the central government. In other words, food scarcity is not a localized problem afflicting

"New Solutions to Old Problems: Food Security in China and Canadian Agri-Innovation," by Linda Qian, Asia Pacific Foundation of Canada, September 22, 2016. Reprinted by permission.

the most vulnerable of populations, but rather the safety and nutritional value of food put on the dinner table is a real concern for the country's entire population, regardless of socioeconomic status and background.

Based on the FAO's official definition, food security includes a country's ability to provide its people with safe food, satisfy each person's essential nutritional needs, and install resilient and sustainable food production systems. For China, one of the biggest challenges currently confronting the country's food security situation is rooted quite literally in China's soil.

China's Soil: Contamination from Farm to Table

Smog usually takes centre stage during discussions of China's pollution or environmental challenges. However, creeping right behind the rising severity of China's poor air quality is the deterioration of the country's water and land; over 80% of ground water in China is contaminated by heavy industries and industrial farming. At the same time, it is these polluting industries and farms that rely on these now-heavily polluted water sources. This has led to the contamination of China's arable land and by extension, the penetration of pollutants into the food chain.

An official study conducted from 2005-2013 showed that 19.4% of all China's arable lands have been heavily contaminated by toxic heavy metals including arsenic, nickel, cadmium, and lead. Proximity of farmlands to contaminated water wells and heavy industries has caused the bioaccumulation of inorganic pollutants in the soil, pollutants that are then absorbed by food crops. Not only does this have an irreversible effect on the ecological vitality of arable lands, but it also produces lasting effects to human health when contaminated crops are consumed.

In 2013, rice crops produced in Hunan Province were found to be heavily tainted by cadmium, a toxic metal linked to kidney failure and skeletal problems. The toxins, products of industrial pollution, made their way into waterways that were diverted into surrounding rice paddies. When news broke about the contamination, all rice imports from Hunan were banned in Guangdong Province, formerly the largest domestic consumer of Hunan-grown rice. Up until 2014, 11% of China's rice production came from Hunan, meaning that the now infamous "rice scandal" was a concern for consumers countrywide, as well as a detriment to the livelihoods of Hunan's rice farmers.

China Daily reported that the area of contaminated land in 2013 was the same size as Belgium. This sounded alarms for the central government, as the total amount of arable lands still safe for farming barely skimmed the national food security "red-line." A dilemma that the central government faces is whether to continue growing crops on tainted soil and risk another "rice scandal," or to allow the contaminated farms to lie fallow and risk a decrease in agricultural yields.

For years, the central government has equated food security with food self-sufficiency—to ensure that China can produce enough staple grains to feed its own people. But over time, environmental concerns—and not to mention, the large quantities of grain demanded by China's growing industrial meat production industries—have caused major revisions to Beijing's grain output and food import targets. In alleviating the burden of the approaching "red-line," the task of securing safe grains and other foodstuff could benefit from looking beyond traditional food systems and agricultural practices, and towards more sustainable and innovative technologies of food production.

Collaboration and Innovation: Canada's Strengths

China's recent acquisition of Syngenta and decision to formulate a law on genetically modified (GM) foods indicates that the country is looking increasingly to innovate itself out of its food production challenges. If properly regulated, GM crops and other agri-chem innovations can play a big role in ensuring seed diversity, crop resiliency, and even environmental regeneration. However, in light of recent high-profile food scandals—such as exploding watermelons and melamine-tainted infant formula—there is understandably a lot of public opposition and mistrust towards "freaky" GM foods and China's agri-chem/agricultural technology sectors in general. Before growing and introducing new crops, the first task is to build confidence and cultivate trust. This culture of trust within China could benefit from the cultivation of stronger bonds beyond China's borders with countries like Canada.

With very strong financial backing by the government, and readily available resources—human, financial, and natural—not to mention a globally renowned reputation in food safety, Canada is already considered a forerunner in agri-foods and agricultural technological innovation. Canadian innovations and initiatives like soil "fingerprinting," and the recent SHAD program on Food Security are examples of how Canada is committed to creating more sustainable solutions to agriculture and food production systems.

In fact, Canada's strengths and influence in these areas are well recognized by Beijing. Many Chinese governmental agencies and ministries—including the Ministry of Agriculture, the Ministry of Science and Technology, and the Ministry of Education—already have well-established ties and partnerships with Ottawa. This has been achieved particularly through what Agriculture and Agri-Foods Canada (AAFC) calls "targeted collaboration." Platforms like the Canada-China Joint Committee on Science and Technology have been facilitating the exchange of knowledge and technological expertise between the two countries, prioritizing research and development in agri-food and genetics and genomes.

Sino-Canadian collaboration has already proven fruitful. One example is the identification of a new "superstar rice crop" by a team of scientists at the University of Toronto and the Chinese Academy of Social Sciences. This "superstar rice crop" has proven to cut down on both pollution and production costs for farmers. According to lead scientist on the project, Dr. Herbert Kronzucker, "everyone wins" with this "responsible plant"—and the potential is there for this discovery to inform new and more sustainable rice-growing strategies in Asia.

Similarly, Canadian farmers have recently begun to grow and market a unique variety of oat as a much more nutritious and environmentally friendly replacement for rice: the Cavena Nuda, otherwise known as the "Rice of the Prairies." In fact, Beijing has bestowed two rare honours on the founder of this oat variety, retired AAFC researcher and Order of Canada recipient, Dr. Vern Burrows. Throughout his career, Dr. Burrows has worked in collaboration with Chinese scientists and agricultural centers to develop oat varieties adapted to different climate and soil conditions, creating economic opportunities for local farmers and improving food security. Known as Dr. Oats in Canada, and the "second Norman Bethune" to China, Dr. Burrows has helped strengthen ties between China and Canada through agricultural innovation and international scientific collaboration.

Food insecurity is a challenge that impacts all countries, including Canada, and working towards achieving food security requires the collective effort of all communities and economies. In light of Canada's strengths in the sector perhaps now is the time for Canada to revamp its global food security strategy to help create more resilient food systems in China and beyond, and to help move the global community one step closer to achieving a world with "Zero Hunger."

3

A Food-Secure Africa

Raphael Obonyo

Raphael Obonyo is a native of Kenya who was selected to the United Nations Habitat's Youth Advisory Board in 2012, where he later served as a special advisor. Obonyo currently serves on multiple international boards, including the Global Diplomatic Forum and the World Bank's Global Coordination Board on Youth and Anti-Corruption.

In the following viewpoint, Raphael Obonyo details Africa's agricultural potential and its impact on the continent's ability to both feed itself and spur socio-economic growth. Obonyo details the continent's emphasis on large-scale commercial farms versus the tens of thousands of smaller farms, and how independently owned farms in many countries do not see the same benefits as the major commercial farms. The viewpoint discusses Africa's response to the food shortages facing the country of Ethiopia, which loses 20 percent of its total crop yield due to poor post-harvest handling.

Development experts and political leaders agree that Africa's enormous agricultural potential, if tapped, can feed the continent and spur socio-economic growth.

In its 2016–2025 strategy for agricultural transformation in Africa, the African Development Bank (AfDB) advises

"Towards a food-secure Africa," by Raphael Obonyo, United Nations Africa Renewal, December 2017-March 2018. Reprinted by permission.

governments to empower smallholder farmers to sustainably and profitably produce more food and achieve a food-secure continent.

That means strengthening the bargaining power of small-scale farmers and giving them access to improved soil that will increase yields, fertilizer and markets to enhance their incomes and well-being.

At a ministerial roundtable in the margins of the 2016 Korea-Africa Economic Cooperation Conference in Seoul, South Korea, AfDB's president Akinwumi Adesina said, "To achieve food sufficiency and turn the continent into a net food exporter, Africa must empower smallholder farmers, who constitute 70% of the population and produce 80% of the food consumed in the continent."

Bukar Tijani, the assistant director-general and regional representative for Africa at the UN's Food and Agricultureal Organizsation (FAO), reinforces that "the key to Africa's food security lies in the smallholder farmer."

Africa is home to more than half of the world's unused arable land, but the continent remains food insecure, with millions of people experiencing chronic hunger and facing famine, according to the Alliance for a Green Revolution in Africa (AGRA), an organization that provides support to small-scale farmers, in its Africa Agriculture Status Report 2017.

In addition to helping smallholder farmers, governments and other stakeholders need to look at ways of empowering youth with knowledge, skills and other resources. According to Agnes Kalibata, the president of AGRA, it is important to "invest in modern technologies and give the youth and women more resources to venture into productive agriculture."

For Alex Awiti, the director at the East African Institute, a policy research organisation, the key to food security is to develop policies and strategies that address the needs of smallholder farmers. Agricultural policies are not in short supply on the continent; the problem has always been the implementation of policies.

"Improving agricultural productivity is a complex public policy problem—it is influenced by a number of complex socio-economic and political factors," says Dr. Awiti.

Factors inhibiting smallholder farmers include the ineffective application of fertilizers; farmers do not use fertilizer deep placement (FDP), which increases yield. In addition, good-quality seeds and fertilizers are often difficult to come by and unaffordable to smallholder farmers even when they can be found.

All of this often leads to low agricultural productivity.

"Fertilizer use in smallholder farms in Africa is 13 to 20 kilogrammes per hectare. This is about a tenth of the global average," explains Dr. Awiti.

Large-Scale Farms

Despite the obvious socio-economic benefits of investing in small-scale farming, African governments prefer to focus on large-scale commercial farms, due to the perceived difficulty of dealing with tens of thousands of smallholder farmers.

"Many smallholder farmers in Ghana farm on poor and degraded soils and lack access to affordable and appropriate inputs, including quality seeds, fertilizers and pesticides," says Kofi Yeboah, a young Ghanaian entrepreneur. These farmers are now calling on their government to subsidize the prohibitive costs of fertilizers.

A small group of Ghanaian companies import fertilizers to the country and further negotiate with the government to set prices. Farmers in remote areas complain that fertilizers do not reach them.

In South Africa, smallholder farmers do not have adequate access to research and extension services, says Mabine Seabe, who advocates for the empowerment of farmers. Worse, they lack strong negotiation skills and information about prices. All of this means that South African smallholder farmers do not receive optimal earnings for their produce. Even when farmers have the right information regarding prices, they are unable to access the big markets and are therefore compelled to sell their produce to middlemen who own distributive networks and make most of the profit.

"Small-scale farmers and the youth do not receive necessary funding and support from government and financial institutions due partly to high risks associated with farming," says Mr. Seabe, adding that government has been slow to enact land reforms and redistribution policies. Land reforms are a difficult issue: only Zimbabwe has implemented them, and it was a politically and racially charged undertaking.

Maputo Declaration

Ethiopia is facing food shortages caused by drought. Meanwhile, over 20% of the total crop yield in Ethiopia is lost to poor post-harvest handling (PHL). To address this problem in Ethiopia, Shayashone, a nonprofit organization dealing in agricultural logistics, strategy and business model development, among other things, is supporting smallholder farmers with storage technology. Yared Sasa, the head of the organization, says, "Farmers need adequate new technology and capacity building to mitigate crop damage during storage by pests."

Shayashone has partnered with Cooperatives for Change (C4C), a nonprofit international development organization from Netherlands, to promote in Ethiopia's Oromia region the use of an improved storage bag created by the PICS (Purdue Improved Crop Storage) project.

Despite multiple constraints faced by African small-scale farmers, government investment in agriculture has doubled since 2010, the Brookings Institution, a US-based nonprofit public policy organization, reported this year. But such investments are still less than 2% of national budgets—far below the 10% threshold African leaders agreed to invest in the sector in their Maputo Declaration in 2003.

In 2017, 14 years after the Maputo Declaration, most countries have not yet met the 10% target. The few that have met the target include Ethiopia, Madagascar, Malawi, Mali and Namibia.

Mr. Tijani of FAO advises African governments and other investors in agriculture to raise awareness among the youth of the benefits of agriculture and how its value chains work. Young people should not engage in farming only for lack of better opportunities; they need to be aware that it is a gainful occupation, he says, adding, "African youth can be powerful drivers of change to lift themselves and others out of poverty, hunger and malnutrition." Unfortunately, many don't consider agriculture a potentially lucrative venture.

About 200 million Africans are between the ages of 15 and 24, and these young people are an untapped reservoir for spurring growth in the agri-food sector. Governments should give them property rights, farming and digital technologies, and other value-chain opportunities, says Mr. Awiti. "This will place them at the nerve center of agricultural e-commerce."

Yara International, an organization fighting famine globally, helped create the Southern Agricultural Corridor of Tanzania (SAGCOT), an ambitious government-led public-private initiative aiming to revitalize 300,000 square kilometers of arable land. The initiative is expected to boost the incomes of thousands of farmers.

Over the last decade, the Tanzanian government has encouraged investment in commercial rice, sugar and maize farming and processing facilities. "This created ready markets for produce, as government targets, supports and links rice farmers to the market," says James Craske, Yara's country manager in Kenya.

Already the anticipated increase in productivity has triggered a demand for more fertilizers. To meet such demand, Yara set up a $26 million fertilizer terminal in the capital, Dar es Salaam, even as the organization and Tanzania's government are working with local banks to provide financing for farmers. The model will create thousands of new jobs and raise incomes for millions of farmers.

The Tanzanian model addresses food insecurity, youth unemployment and socio-economic exclusions. It can potentially spur rural development. However, the model has been criticized for destroying state-owned mangroves that provided food security for many citizens.

Head of the Africa Progress Panel and former UN secretary-general Kofi Annan believes that Africa can close the productivity gap in the agriculture value chain. "Africa's smallholder farmers are more than capable of feeding the continent as long as they make use of the latest agronomic practices in combination with appropriately adapted seeds and fertilizers to boost their crop yield."

The question remains: How far and how quickly are African governments willing to go to empower smallholder farmers to achieve the goal of a food-secure continent?

<h1>4</h1>

What Are Food Deserts?

Robyn Correll

Robyn Correll is a public health professional with over a decade of experience providing science-based information and training on a variety of topics, including vaccines and vaccine-preventable diseases, reproductive health, and cancer prevention.

In the following viewpoint, Robyn Correll details what is considered to be a food desert, and specifically what food deserts are in the United States. According to the US Department of Agriculture, there are more than 23 million people in the United States who live in areas without access to a supermarket or another similar store that sells affordable healthy food options. One major impact is socioeconomic status, in that it is easier for a family with a higher income to afford more fresh foods and vegetables, which have a higher nutritional value compared to less expensive foods.

What you eat and how much can have a huge impact on your longterm health. Healthy eating habits are important to prevent a long list of ailments, which is why health officials for decades have encouraged families to eat more nutritious foods like fruits and vegetables and avoid junk or processed foods like chips and fast food cheeseburgers.

But for many families in the United States, it's not that simple. According to the U.S. Department of Agriculture, more than 23 million people in the United States live in areas without access to supermarkets or other stores selling a variety of affordable healthy food options. These communities, known as food deserts, are a serious environmental health issue that can impact the lives of families for generations.

Definition

While there's no one standard definition to go by, food deserts are generally considered to be places where residents don't have access to affordable nutritious foods like fruits, vegetables and whole grains. Instead of grocery stores or farmers markets, these areas often have convenience stores and gas stations with limited shelf space available for healthy options—making nutritious foods virtually inaccessible for many families there.

But accessibility can be relative, and proximity to a store is only one factor of many that influences a person's ability to eat healthily. Income and resources (like transportation) can also keep people from being able to access healthy food options. For example, two neighbors might each live a mile from a grocery store, but one has a car while the other relies on public transit. The neighbor who drives regularly will likely have more options when it comes to groceries than his friend next door.

Socioeconomic status might also play a role, as low-income individuals get priced out of high-quality health foods. After all, $50 worth of boxed meals and frozen dinners can often last a family longer than $50 worth of fresh vegetables and lean meats. They're also quicker and easier to prepare—something that matters a lot when parents work multiple jobs or long hours to make ends meet.

Because of this, pinning down what precisely constitutes a food desert can be challenging. For its part, the USDA hammered out a few parameters in its investigations to determine whether an area had limited access to healthy food. It classified an urban area as a food desert if it was more than 0.5 or one mile away from a supermarket, grocery store or other sources of healthy, affordable food, and rural communities were those located 10 or 20 miles away. But the department also looked at other factors beyond location, such as low-income status and access to a vehicle.

Locations

When most public health officials talk about food deserts, they're often referring to urban environments—inner cities where higher property costs can scare away many potential grocers. But while roughly 82 percent of food deserts are in urban areas, rural communities aren't exactly exempt. According to the USDA, an estimated 335,000 people in the United States live more than 20 miles from a supermarket.

Food deserts exist all over the country, but they are more common in the South and Midwest, with lower income states like Louisiana or Mississippi seeing a disproportionately high percentage of the population lacking access to healthy food, compared to states like Oregon or New Hampshire.

Lower income areas, in general, are typically the hardest hit by food deserts. According to a USDA study, moderate and high-income areas had more than 24,000 large grocery stores and supermarkets in 2015, while low-income census tracts had just 19,700. In fact, half of all low-income zip codes (that is, where the median income is under $25,000) qualify as food deserts.

Who Lives There

Low-income individuals—especially those without access to a car or who live in remote rural areas—often have the hardest time getting healthy foods. For these individuals, obtaining healthy food means driving further to get them. That is, of course, if driving is even an option. More than two million households located in food deserts don't have a vehicle, according to the USDA.

Residents of urban food deserts also pay more for groceries than families in the suburbs. By one estimate, they pay up to 37 percent more for the *same exact products*, typically because of higher operating and shipping costs inside the city. Lower-income families already put a larger percentage of their paychecks toward buying groceries, but living in a food desert means that paycheck won't stretch nearly as far as it would have in areas where fresh fruits, vegetables, and proteins are more accessible. When faced with those obstacles, it's no surprise that some families opt for the less-healthy—but much more affordable—options available to them.

Relative to other areas, food deserts are also more likely to have:

- Smaller populations
- Lower levels of education among residents
- Higher unemployment rates
- Higher rates of vacant homes
- Higher concentrations of minority residents

It should be noted that living in a food desert isn't the same as being food insecure. Not everyone who lives in a food desert lacks access to healthy foods. Making the trip to a big store or having groceries delivered is typically still an option for those who have the means and opportunity to do so. Likewise, a person doesn't have to reside in a food desert to lack access to things like whole grains and fresh produce. In some cases, such foods might be available, but high prices make them unaffordable to some. Food insecurity is a very real issue that, while more common in food deserts, isn't limited to them.

Impact on Health

The biggest health concern linked to food deserts is, ironically, obesity. And that makes sense, given that people who can't easily access healthy foods tend to eat less healthily than people who can. Unhealthy eating habits lead to weight gain, and that, in turn, leads to obesity.

Being significantly overweight or obese increases a person's risk for all kinds of health issues, including diabetes, heart disease, stroke and high blood pressure. Being obese during pregnancy can also up your chances of complications like gestational diabetes, preeclampsia, birth defects and miscarriage. Excessive weight may even increase your risk of cancer, with one study estimating a jaw-dropping 481,000 new cases of cancer worldwide in 2012 were due to being overweight or obese. The impact has the potential to last for generations, too, as kids of obese parents are more likely to become obese themselves.

Beyond just obesity, unhealthy eating habits in the first few years life can also significantly affect a child's ability to grow. Brains and bodies develop quickly during early childhood, and to do that, they need key ingredients. Not getting enough foods rich in things like iron, vitamin A or iodine has been linked to cognitive difficulties, weaker immune systems, and stunted growth.

It's not just child nutrition that matters either. Babies born to women who don't get enough folate in the early stages of pregnancy have a higher risk of being born with potentially serious birth defects. Decades of nutrition research have found that unhealthy eating habits can have severe—and sometimes lifelong—consequences, which is why health officials are concerned about so many people living in areas with poor access to healthy foods.

Another oft-overlooked concern about food deserts is the risk posed to those with dietary restrictions and food allergies. An estimated 15 million people in the United States have a food allergy (some more than one), many of which can be life-threatening. Roughly 200,000 people a year have to receive emergency medical treatment because they ate or drank something they were allergic to. Not being able to buy food that they know is safe can force people to take unnecessary risks in order to feed themselves and their families.

That said, while studies have found significant links between a community's lack of supermarkets to health issues like obesity, recent research is also beginning to signal that that relationship might be a whole lot more complicated than was previously believed. Low income and education have both been linked to obesity outside of the context of food deserts, and some recent studies have concluded that socioeconomic status might play a more important role in nutritional outcomes than proximity to a grocery store.

What Can Be Done?

Food deserts have been on the radar at public health departments for a while now, and many have already begun implementing strategies and policies to bring produce and other healthy foods to food deserts. The CDC recommends several strategies to address and prevent food deserts, including:

- Building community gardens
- Establishing local farmers markets
- Improving public transportation from food deserts to established markets
- Tweaking local laws and tax codes to entice supermarkets and other healthy food retailers to set up shop

But making affordable healthy food easier to access is only part of the solution. By one estimate, providing low-income neighborhoods with access to higher quality food would only drop nutritional inequality by nine percent. That's because while opening up supermarkets in former food deserts might bring healthier food options to the neighborhood, it doesn't magically change food-buying habits. Neither does families moving to a place where healthy eating is the norm and health foods are abundant.

Families get into a groove of what they like to eat and how much they like to spend on groceries. As many parents can attest, it takes a while to find a menu of things the whole family can enjoy, and disrupting that routine will take a whole lot more than building a store nearby. Helping communities gain closer access to more affordable healthy food options is an important step, but it should be accompanied by efforts to change eating behaviors, too, through expanded nutrition education.

Food is a deeply cultural and personal thing. Many families have beloved meals that give them comfort and make them feel at home, and religions often incorporate food into their celebrations and rituals. In order to bring about any meaningful change, nutrition education should be created with these traditions in mind, being careful to acknowledge deeply rooted cultural norms found in every community.

Any efforts to combat the issue of food deserts and nutrition deficits should also be practical for the community they're targeting. Encouraging families to participate in a community garden, for example, might not be feasible in an area where many of the adults work multiple jobs with minimal free time to pitch in.

Food Deserts vs. Food Swamps

In light of what we know about food deserts, some researchers investigating nutritional gaps are shifting focus away from a lack of healthy food options and instead zeroing in on an abundance of unhealthy ones. These areas—dubbed "food swamps"—don't just lack grocery stores; they are also crammed full of fast food places and convenience stores.

Studies have shown that the presence of these areas is linked to a poorer diet and is possibly an even stronger predictor of obesity rates than a lack of supermarkets, as the in-your-face presence of unhealthy meal options virtually cancels out any benefits adding grocery stores might bring.

This has encouraged many health agencies to take a different approach to food deserts and swamps by adapting the existing environment to make healthy choices easier to make. Instead of trying to attract grocery stores, some cities have tried to go where people already do their grocery shopping and urge corner stores and gas stations to spend more shelf space on affordable, fresh produce. Others have set up mobile farmers markets that resemble food trucks to drive out to low-access areas so that residents don't have to go out of their way to buy healthy food.

A Word from Verywell

The key to addressing both food deserts and food swamps is to acknowledge that every community is different and, therefore, will likely need a unique combination of strategies. Opening up a grocery store in every neighborhood can sound good in theory but might be impractical or unnecessary in practice. Helping families find healthy, affordable and practical meals will likely require some innovative solutions, but it is essential to maintaining and improving the health of communities for generations to come.

5

America's Food Deserts

The Week Publications, Inc.

The Week Publications, Inc. owns the Week, *a weekly news magazine with editions in the United Kingdom, the United States, and Australia that provides perspectives on current events as well as editorial commentary from multiple political perspectives.*

The following viewpoint details the growing trend of food deserts in the United States. Defining a food desert as a community in which residents must travel at least a mile to buy fresh food, these can be found in rural areas in West Virginia, Ohio, and Kentucky, but also urban locations like Detroit, Chicago, and New York City. Food deserts have also been linked to the United States' obesity crisis, as people in these locations are often forced to depend on processed and fast food rather than fresh food.

What is a food desert? A community in which residents must travel at least a mile to buy fresh meat, dairy products, and vegetables. More precisely, the U.S. Department of Agriculture (USDA) defines a food desert as any census district where at least 20 percent of the inhabitants are below the poverty line and 33 percent live over a mile from the nearest supermarket (or in rural areas, more than 10 miles). Approximately 23.5 million Americans live in a food desert, says the USDA, including vast, rural swaths of West Virginia, Ohio, and Kentucky, as well as urban

"America's 'food deserts,'" The Week Publications Inc., August 12, 2011. Reprinted by permission.

areas like Detroit, Chicago, and New York City. The government believes food deserts are contributing to the obesity epidemic in the U.S., by forcing the rural and urban poor to rely on processed foods and fast food, instead of fresh meat, vegetables, and fruit. Today, more than one third of adult Americans are obese.

Can This Trend Be Reversed?

The government thinks it can, if major supermarkets open stores in blighted areas and stock affordable healthy food options. First Lady Michelle Obama's "Let's Move!" campaign, which aims to reduce childhood obesity, has taken a lead role in this effort, and recently scored a major coup by convincing Walmart, SuperValu, and Walgreens to open or expand 1,500 grocery stores in food deserts. The involvement of large retail firms has "the potential to be a game-changer for kids and communities all across this country," Obama said. "More parents will have a fresh food retailer right in their community, so they can feed their families the way they want." But not everyone shares the First Lady's optimism; in fact, some critics say opening new stores and markets in so-called food deserts will have little or no impact on how people eat.

Why Would That Be?

First of all, the critics say, the very concept of a food desert may be a mirage. One recent University of Washington study found that only 15 percent of people shop for groceries within their own census areas; most of us, in other words, are accustomed to traveling a few miles to stock our pantries. Critics also point out that the USDA takes only supermarkets into account when deciding whether an area is a food desert. Smaller grocery stores, farmers markets, and roadside stalls aren't included. Moreover, the vast majority of households (93 percent) in food deserts have access to a car, and can easily drive to grocery stores over a mile from their homes.

So What's the Real Problem?

Many people simply like fast food better. A recent University of North Carolina (UNC) study of the eating habits of 5,000 people over 15 years found that living near a supermarket had little impact on whether people had healthy diets. But living close to fast-food outlets did. The real problem, the study found, is the existence of "food swamps," filled with convenience stores selling calorie-loaded packaged foods, gallon cups of soda, and other sugar-loaded beverages, and fast-food chains peddling burgers, fries, and fried chicken on almost every street corner. That's no exaggeration: There are now five fast-food restaurants for every supermarket in the U.S.

Why Do People Choose the "Bad" Food?

Fast food is generally cheaper, and doesn't need to be prepared and cooked, so it's more convenient. Studies have also shown that the huge jolt of fat, salt, and sugar fast food delivers can be almost as addictive as hard drugs (see below). Then there's the advertising factor: Fast-food companies spend about $4.2 billion a year marketing their products as life's ultimate rewards, through saliva-producing ads depicting cheese-and-pepperoni-covered pizzas, juicy double cheeseburgers, and steaming French fries.

Can These Preferences Be Changed?

The UNC study suggests using zoning laws to restrict the number of fast-food restaurants in low-income neighborhoods. Los Angeles has already experimented with this approach, having imposed a one-year moratorium on the building of fast-food restaurants over a 32-square-mile area. City officials say the results were successful, and have now imposed permanent zoning restrictions on fast-food chains in the poorer, southern part of the city. "We have already attracted new sit-down restaurants, full-service grocery stores, and healthy food alternatives," said City Councilwoman Jan Perry. "Ultimately, this action is about providing choices."

Will People Choose Healthy Food?

Not necessarily. Many Americans have little experience eating or preparing broccoli, asparagus, and other produce; in fact, only 26 percent of the nation's adults now eat three servings of vegetables a day. The poor, in particular, have become so accustomed to salty packaged foods and sugary beverages that they find fresh food bland, strange, and off-putting. "It's simplistic thinking that if you put fruits and vegetables there, they'll buy it," said Barry Popkin, author of the UNC study. "You have to encourage it, you need advertising, you need support." Changing Americans' diets, in other words, won't be as simple as telling them to eat their peas.

Fast Food Junkies

If it sometimes seems that Americans are addicted to fast food, it might be that we actually are. Studies have repeatedly found that the consequences of bingeing on high-calorie, high-fat foods mimic the effects of drug addiction. A recent study by the Scripps Research Institute found that gorging on fast food actually changes the brain's chemical makeup, making it more difficult to trigger the release of dopamine (aka "the pleasure chemical"). That means fast-food addicts need to eat more and more to feel happy—the same way users of cocaine and other drugs, for example, need to keep upping their dosages to get high. An earlier study, by Princeton University, found that rats who were fed and then withdrawn from a high-fat, high-sugar diet exhibited similar symptoms—chattering teeth and the shakes—to junkies going cold turkey. "Drugs give a bigger effect," said study author Bart Hoebel, "but it's essentially the same process."

6

The Real Problem with Food Deserts

Food Empowerment Project

The Food Empowerment Project is a volunteer-based nonprofit organization that seeks to create a more just and sustainable world by recognizing the power of one's food choices, especially in low-income areas.

The following viewpoint showcases the true issues with food deserts in the United States. One of the primary issues is that it is not possible to determine exactly how many people are located in food deserts. Considering the problems with the way the North American Industry Classification System (NAICS) categorizes retail outlets that sell food, it is possible that places that actually are food deserts may go overlooked. Many residents of urban centers live in what could reasonably be considered food deserts.

Food Empowerment Project (F.E.P.) recognizes the problem with the term food desert, defined by the USDA as mostly being about proximity to food providers, rather than considering other factors such as racism, cost of living, people being time poor and cash poor, cultural appropriateness of available foods, the ability of people to grow their owns foods, etc. F.E.P. considers terms like food apartheid and food oppression to be more accurate, but since food desert is the term that is most commonly used, we have kept it as our title.

"Food Deserts," by Food Empowerment Project, foodispower.org. Reprinted by permission.

Food deserts can be described as geographic areas where residents' access to affordable, healthy food options (especially fresh fruits and vegetables) is restricted or nonexistent due to the absence of grocery stores within convenient travelling distance. For instance, according to a report prepared for Congress by the Economic Research Service of the US Department of Agriculture, about 2.3 million people (or 2.2 percent of all US households) live more than one mile away from a supermarket and do not own a car. In urban areas, access to public transportation may help residents overcome the difficulties posed by distance, but economic forces have driven grocery stores out of many cities in recent years, making them so few and far between that an individual's food shopping trip may require taking several buses or trains. In suburban and rural areas, public transportation is either very limited or unavailable, with supermarkets often many miles away from people's homes.

The other defining characteristic of food deserts is socio-economic: that is, they are most commonly found in black and brown communities and low-income areas (where many people don't have cars). Studies have found that wealthy districts have three times as many supermarkets as poor ones do, that white neighborhoods contain an average of four times as many supermarkets as predominantly black ones do, and that grocery stores in African-American communities are usually smaller with less selection. People's choices about what to eat are severely limited by the options available to them and what they can afford—and many food deserts contain an overabundance of fast food chains selling cheap "meat" and dairy-based foods that are high in fat, sugar and salt. Processed foods (such as snack cakes, chips and soda) typically sold by corner delis, convenience stores and liquor stores are usually just as unhealthy.

Food Empowerment Project's report, "Shining a Light on the Valley of Heart's Delight," shows that it is possible to overlook communities that are located in food deserts when relying on data collected by the US government. We found that, "Part of the problem is how the US government's North American Industry

Classification System (NAICS is the standard used by the federal statistical agencies in classifying business establishments) categorizes retail outlets that sell food. According to the NAICS code, small corner grocery stores are statistically lumped together with supermarkets, such as Safeway, Whole Foods Market, etc. In other words, a community with no supermarket and two corner grocery stores that offer liquor and food would be counted as having two retail food outlets even though the food offered may be extremely limited and consist mainly of junk food."

In addition to this, we found that many of the convenience stores that had items such as a bunch of bananas or a few apples would sell the fruits individually. Because these items are not priced, the customers are often at the mercy of the person behind the counter who determines the cost then and there. Customers who don't have a good understanding of English might never ask the price of the item.

Those living in food deserts may also find it difficult to locate foods that are culturally appropriate for them, and dietary restrictions, such as lactose intolerance, gluten allergies, etc., also limit the food choices of those who do not have access to larger chain stores that have more selection. Additionally, studies have found that urban residents who purchase groceries at small neighborhood stores pay between 3 and 37 percent more than suburbanites buying the same products at supermarkets.

Healthier foods are generally more expensive than unhealthful foods, particularly in food deserts. For instance, while the overall price of fruits and vegetables in the US increased by nearly 75 percent between 1989 and 2005, the price of fatty foods dropped by more than 26 percent during the same period. While such inflation has strained the food budgets of many families regardless of their financial status, the higher cost of healthy foods often puts them entirely beyond the monetary means of many lower-income people.

While unhealthy eating may be economically cheaper in the short-term, the consequences of long-term constrained access to healthy foods is one of the main reasons that ethnic minority and low-income populations suffer from statistically higher rates of obesity, type 2 diabetes, cardiovascular disease, and other diet-related conditions than the general population.

Whatever their age, obesity puts people at a greater risk for serious, even fatal health disorders (particularly coronary heart disease and diabetes, the first and seventh leading causes of death in the US respectively):

The incidence of diabetes among US adults doubled between 1996 and 2007, and "type 2 diabetes" (a variant of the disease that is often caused by obesity) may account for 90 to 95 percent of these cases. Only twenty years ago, type 2 diabetes was virtually unknown among people under 40 years old, but in the past decade it has increased tenfold among adolescents (mirroring this age group's escalating obesity rates). While the incidence of type 2 diabetes has risen across demographic lines in recent years, the greatest increases have occurred among black and brown communities. The highest rates of escalation have been identified in Native American youth and African-Americans and Latinos of all age groups, with these groups suffering disproportionately higher rates of type 2 diabetes compared to whites. These are also the groups most likely to live in food deserts, and researchers have established a strong correlation between food insecurity and increased diabetes rates. One study of Chicago neighborhoods found the death rate from diabetes in food deserts to be twice that of areas offering access to grocery stores, while another conducted in California found that adults ages 50 and over from black and brown communities had double the diabetes rate of whites from the same age demographic. Researchers explain this disparity by emphasizing that the high-calorie foods most readily available in food deserts put residents living in these areas at greater risk for diabetes in the first place, and that having restricted access to healthy foods also makes it harder for them to manage diabetes once they are diagnosed.

Heart disease causes more than 2.4 million deaths in the US every year. One of the main causes of cardiovascular disease is a diet high in unhealthy fats and low-density lipoprotein (LDL) cholesterol—typified by the types of fare commonly available in food deserts. Just as African-Americans are statistically more likely than other populations to live in food deserts, heart disease kills more blacks every year than whites (despite the fact that whites make up almost 80 percent of the total US populace, and blacks comprise slightly more than 13 percent). Even children and adolescents living in food deserts are at greater risk for cardiovascular disease (both now and when they reach adulthood) due to the increased prevalence of obesity in those communities.

Food for Thought

Public awareness of the formidable problems posed by food deserts is growing, thanks largely to the efforts of community activists, entrepreneurs and government officials committed to increasing people's access to healthy food options. On the national level, First Lady Michelle Obama has spearheaded the "Let's Move" campaign to combat childhood obesity, which includes a goal of eradicating food deserts by 2017 with a $400 million investment from the government focused on providing tax breaks to supermarkets that open in food deserts. Many urban areas are also implementing initiatives locally to solve their food desert challenges.

- **Chicago**—More than 500,000 residents (mostly African-American) live in food deserts, and an additional 400,000 live in neighborhoods with a preponderance of fast food restaurants and no grocery stores nearby. Some food justice activists have sought to close this gap by opening food co-ops in underserved areas where supermarkets have historically been unsuccessful. In addition to selling fresh and organic fruits and vegetables, bulk whole grains and beans, and soy-based meat substitutes, some of these stores (like Fresh Family Foods on the city's South Side) also offer cooking and nutrition classes to educate the public about making healthy food choices.
- **Los Angeles**—In 2008, the Los Angeles City Council voted to enact a moratorium on new fast food outlets in a 32-square-mile zone encompassing some of South L.A.'s most arid food

deserts, an area where about 97 percent of the population is either Latino, African-American, or of mixed race. Having fewer fast food restaurants created greater demand for more and better food choices, so Councilmembers subsequently passed another measure offering grocery stores and sit-down restaurants serving healthier meals financial incentives to open up in underserved communities. These policies have so far succeeded in bringing the first new supermarket to South L.A. in about a decade.

- **New York City**—An estimated 750,000 New York City residents live in food deserts, while about three million people live in places where stores that sell fresh produce are few or far away. Supermarkets throughout New York City have closed down in recent years due to increasing rents and shrinking profit margins, but the disappearance of urban grocery stores has had the most serious impact on low-income communities, especially those that are predominantly African-American (such East/Central Harlem and North/Central Brooklyn). To fill this void, the city started its Green Carts program, which has been bringing affordable fresh fruits and vegetables to underserved areas while providing jobs for vendors since 2008. Hundreds of Green Carts are already on the streets in food deserts, and that number is rapidly increasing as prospective vendors obtain training, licenses and permits from the city.

What Can I Do If I Live in a Food Desert?

If you recognize that you are living in a food desert, you can start by helping those in your community understand what this means and talk about ways to make change. Discussing different options, such as growing your own food, working with local retailers to sell healthy, vegan foods, etc. is a good place to start. It is also important to bring your ideas and concerns to policy makers—city councilmembers, state legislators, etc.

To learn more you can also reach out to others who have worked on this issue.

7

The Native American Connection to Food Deserts

Amy McDermott

Amy McDermott is a science journalist who currently writes for Front Matter, *the magazine section of the Proceedings of the National Academy of Sciences of the United States of America.*

The following viewpoint goes deep into the issue of food deserts in the United States by focusing on systemic poverty and the lack of access to fresh foods in Native American communities. McDermott showcases the variety of Native American cuisines in North America prior to the arrival of European colonists and how some are attempting to return to this more nutritious diet. In America's largest reservation, the 25,000 square miles spanning Arizona, New Mexico, and Utah, there are only ten grocery stores for an area the size of West Virginia.

Andromeda Na'lniitr'e'sdvm Lopez grew up on canned meat, canned juice, white flour, and evaporated milk. It was common fare for her tribe, the Tolowa Dee-ni'. But at 21, Lopez had a diabetes scare while pregnant and knew her diet had to change.

"I didn't want to continue eating the way I was raised," she says. Lopez, now 30, is a single mom in the far northwestern corner of California, where the Tolowa Dee-ni''s traditional home is cut into a quiltwork of reservation, county, and city land. She tries

"Many Native Americans lack access to healthy food, but there's a growing movement to change that," by Amy McDermott, Grist Magazine, Inc., January 31, 2017. Reprinted by permission.

her best to include vegetables in every meal, but Lopez says, "it can get expensive."

In almost any Native American community, you'll find people like Lopez struggling with similar, systemic problems. One-in-four live in poverty, according to census data. Native Americans are twice as likely as white people to lack access to safe, healthy foods—ultimately leading to obesity and diabetes.

That's why on Wednesday afternoons in the summer, Lopez drives five miles down a two-lane highway, past cow pastures and lily fields, to a garden planted on tribal land in the town of Smith River, California. It's a beautiful place to put your hands in the soil; mountains and redwoods rise on one side, while fields give way to an ocean view on the other.

Lopez weeds and harvests along with other volunteers, and in return, takes home about 10 pounds of tomatoes, squash, pumpkins, and peas every week. She plans meals, like soups and stir fries, around those veggies.

In Del Norte, the Tolowa Dee-ni' and community food council (a group that organizes around healthy eating) are expanding community gardens. So far, they've funneled more than 1,000 pounds of produce into early learning programs and meals for community elders. This year, they'll create four new food forests by planting dozens of perennials like fruit trees, berry bushes, and traditional crops, with support from the U.S. Department of Agriculture and United Indian Health Services.

Local gardens are a budding solution to the food insecurity that plagues indigenous communities. From California to New Mexico to Maine, Native Americans are growing what they eat, more and more. Climate change makes these efforts especially urgent, says anthropologist Darren Ranco of the University of Maine in Orono. Homegrown fruits and veggies are good for health and a bulwark against a climate-uncertain future.

Recipe for Disaster

Before Europeans arrived in North America, Native American cuisine varied greatly from location to location. Lopez's people relied on the abundance of the Pacific coast: elk and deer, salmon and smelt, berries and acorns. But as Native Americans were violently displaced by Europeans, many of those food traditions were lost.

"When you pick up a people and forcibly remove them … you're disconnecting all those connections with food," says attorney Janie Hipp, former senior advisor for tribal relations to President Obama's Agriculture Secretary, Tom Vilsack.

Making matters worse, grocery stores are hard to come by in the remote and isolated areas often allotted to Native Americans. The U.S. government does provide monthly supplies, but reservations stay mired in poverty and dependent on outside forces for food.

"A lot of our food does come from the likes of a Walmart Supercenter," says Zach Ducheneaux of the Cheyenne River Sioux Indian Reservation in Eagle Butte, South Dakota. Out there, three grocery stores and a handful of fast food joints serve a region the size of Connecticut. "Save up to afford a ride to town," he says, "fill up the back of the truck with cheap food."

The problem is perhaps starkest on America's largest reservation. Across the 25,000 square miles of Arizona, New Mexico, and Utah that comprise The Navajo Nation, three-quarters of households are food insecure (the highest rates in the country). People eat at gas stations and quick-e-marts. There are only 10 grocery stores for an area the size of West Virginia.

California's Tolowa Dee-ni' Nation has the same issue. Only two grocery stores serve the community and the rest of Del Norte County. Residents have to drive up to an hour for fruits and vegetables. Convenience marts, with their unhealthy options, are often much closer.

Fixing this problem is going to take a whole lot more than swapping gas station Cheetos for imported bananas, though. "To deal with food insecurity, health, nutrition, and lack of economic development," Hipp says, "we need to look inside these communities, to the land we're standing on."

Growing Change

In northern California, the Tolowa Dee-ni' and larger community are doing just that. Out there, more grocery stores aren't the best option, says Angela Glore of Del Norte's community food council, because people live spread out across 1,300 square miles. Gardens are a better alternative, she says. They provide healthy meals while training local people to grow their own food.

"There's a real interest in learning how to produce your own," says Brittany Rymer, also of the food council. "But those skills have been lost through generations."

Now the Tolowa Dee-ni' are regaining those skills. Two years ago, the nation won a $400,000 USDA grant, scheduled to last through 2019, to expand existing gardens and plant food forests. United Indian Health Services has awarded the Tolowa Dee-ni' another $80,000 so far for gardens and education in the town of Smith River.

In the first summer after they were expanded, the Smith River gardens yielded 600 pounds of fresh fruits and vegetables. And that first winter, they produced 500 pounds of squash. That food went into hot lunches for elders of the Tolowa Dee-ni' Nation and into the kitchens of garden volunteers. Pumpkins and winter squash also went to Smith River's Howonquet Head Start program. Workshops on beekeeping, container gardening, and canning preserves also bring the promise of self-reliance.

Over the next year, the four new food forests will take root at local schools and community institutions. The beauty of food forests, Glore explains, is that once established, they don't need the same daily watering and attention as smaller garden plots. Forests are ultimately low maintenance.

No one knows how much food these gardens will eventually grow, but one semidwarf apple tree can produce up to 400 pounds of fruit a year. Each new garden might have 20 of these trees intermixed with many other species. That's 8,000 pounds of apples annually—just one of many crops—that will feed people like Lopez and her 9-year-old daughter.

"I didn't go out there thinking I was going to get paid in vegetables," Lopez says, laughing. She started volunteering for stress relief and exercise. But the free food has been a financial help. "Not having to spend that extra money," she says, "I could consistently provide those meals for [my daughter]."

Still, entrenched attitudes and eating habits are hard to overcome. When Lopez changed her diet 10 years ago, her family raised a collective eyebrow. And today at community gatherings, the food is still mostly unhealthy, she says. "When you throw a salad out there, [the elders] want to know where the hell the bread is at."

Those old ways of thinking may change as food access improves. But community gardens still won't be a panacea, solving all tribal food woes in all places.

The biggest hurdle for gardens, says horticultural scientist Kevin Lombard of New Mexico State University, is keeping people interested and invested. Not everyone likes working out in the sun and rain. "The culture that we're in now is pretty much fast-paced, fast food," he says. "It's more of a lifestyle issue than anything else."

Gardens aren't the only answer. But they're a start. And homegrown food, Ranco of the University of Maine says, protects health *and* prepares Native American communities to survive climate change. As weird weather threatens food supplies around the country, he says, healthy groceries will be even harder to find in remote and rural areas. Homegrown food is one safety net in a less stable world.

Indigenous peoples are already central in the fights for clean water and against global warming, he says. Food may be next.

8

The Tax on Junk Food

Eliza Barclay

Eliza Barclay is a science and health editor at Vox.com. She was previously the co-editor of NPR's food vertical "The Salt" and covered food, health, and science for NPR on the web and on the air.

This viewpoint showcases how the Navajo Nation was able to not just put a tax on sugary beverages and junk food—a feat more than thirty cities and states across the United States were unable to accomplish—but also on junk food while at the same time making fruits and vegetables more affordable. While there are other cities that have passed legislation of some sort regarding unhealthy foods, the Navajo Nation's are some of the strictest, with the intention of mitigating the health crisis in the community.

M ore than 30 cities and states across the country have attempted to tax soda. Nearly all have failed.

Now, a community of about 250,000 people has found a way to tax not just sugary beverages, but also junk food. At the same time, it's making fresh produce more affordable in one of the hardest regions in the U.S. to buy it.

As of April 1, products like cheese puffs and energy drinks sold inside the Navajo Nation (the 27,000-square-mile reservation extending into Utah, Arizona and New Mexico) will carry an extra

2-cent sales tax (on top of the 5-cent sales tax on most goods sold there). And since October, fresh fruits and vegetables there have been tax-free.

In December, Berkeley, Calif., became the first city in the U.S. to pass a soda tax measure. But the measure that the Navajo Nation Council signed into law in November 2014 goes even further. Known as the Healthy Diné Nation Act, it's the first in the U.S. to tax both sugary beverages and snacks, sweets and baked and fried goods of "minimal-to-no nutritional value."

In December, Berkeley, Calif., became the first city in the U.S. to pass a soda tax measure. But the measure that the Navajo Nation Council signed into law in November 2014 goes even further. Known as the Healthy Diné Nation Act, it's the first in the U.S. to tax both sugary beverages and snacks, sweets and baked and fried goods of "minimal-to-no nutritional value."

Wednesday's implementation of the "junk food tax" was many years in the making, according to the Diné Community Advocacy Alliance, a group made up of volunteers grievously concerned about diabetes and obesity rates on the reservation and beyond. The group, whose name, Diné, is another name for Navajo, led the campaign for the measures.

Some 10 percent of Navajo Nation residents have diabetes, and another 30 percent are pre-diabetic, according to Indian Health Services. The obesity rate within the reservation ranges from 23 to 60 percent.

Health advocates say those alarming rates are partly due to the fact that the reservation is a food desert. The U.S. Department of Agriculture has identified it as such, and local groups have documented both the prevalence of unhealthy foods (some 90 percent of the inventory of local stores) and the limited number of places to shop for food of any kind. The Diné Policy Institute noted in a 2014 report that there are only 10 full-service grocery stores on the entire Navajo reservation.

The idea for the soda and junk-food tax measure was born four years ago, Denisa Livingston, a spokeswoman for DCAA who's also a community health advocate and Navajo tribe member, tells The Salt.

She and other community organizers wanted to find a way to raise money for health and wellness programs, but also make a point about how difficult it is to buy healthy food on the reservation and create new incentives to improve access to it.

"This is the start of making people aware that we are living in a food desert—something that's not normal," says Livingston. "If you [compare] the Bashas' grocery store on the reservation and in Phoenix, looking at the layout, you see they have much more healthy foods available in Phoenix compared to here."

It's unclear how much revenue the junk food and sugary beverage tax will generate between now and 2020, when it expires, but Livingston says it could be as much as $3 million a year. The funds are earmarked for health and wellness programs on the reservation, like gardening and nutrition education.

But Livingston says she also hopes that the lifting of the tax on fruits and vegetables will help raise demand, and in turn, improve the availability of these foods in local markets.

More then half of Navajo members surveyed in 2012 said they travel to off-nation stores to purchase groceries; some said they drove up to 240 miles round trip to buy vegetables and meat.

"With the tax measures, now the Navajo people will have an opportunity to have ownership over healthy foods [that will be cheaper now] and re-create our grocery stores," Livingston says.

Since there's no precedent for a junk food tax anywhere in the U.S., it's unclear what effect the changes will have on eating habits.

"The thing is that people addicted to sugar and junk food would pay any price to get what they want," says Terrol Johnson, a member of the Tohono O'odham tribe in Arizona, co-founder and CEO of Tohono O'odham Community Action and publisher of Native Foodways Magazine. "My hope is that the tax will go back into the community for more education, and to invest in school lunches."

According to Livingston, she and the other organizers faced significant opposition to the measures along the way, including pressure from the beverage industry to drop the soda tax proposal.

"About a year ago, there were beverage companies on the reservation lobbying against the tax," says Danny Simpson, another DCAA representative and tribe member.

What happened on Navajo Nation may be somewhat unique, politically speaking, since it's the only tribe that taxes goods sold on the reservation, says Raymond Foxworth, deputy director of development and senior program officer at the First Nations Development Institute (as well as a Navajo tribe member). His group helped fund efforts to pass the measure.

While other tribes interested in using taxes to combat obesity and diabetes may not be able to replicate it exactly, "this is a great example of how tribes can use their tribal sovereignty" to pass legislation that might not fly elsewhere, Foxworth tells The Salt.

And, Foxworth adds, other tribes may be inspired to try other tactics, like "mandating that food sold at the casino comes from local producers."

Livingston, for one, says she's seeing a lot of momentum in Navajo Nation around healthful eating, thanks to the new tax measures and other initiatives encouraging home and community gardens for growing fresh produce.

And in March, a local non-profit announced a partnership with Wholesome Wave, a Connecticut-based group that connects low-income people with local produce. Using Wholesome Wave's Fruit and Vegetable Prescription Program (which we've reported on) as a model, the collaboration will focus on healthy food access in Navajo Nation and offering chronic disease prevention outreach.

9

Climate Change and Food Insecurity

Carolyn Kenney

Carolyn Kenney is a senior policy analyst for National Security and International Policy at American Progress, working specifically on the Sustainable Security and Peacebuilding Initiative.

Taking food security—and more importantly, food insecurity— to an international level, this viewpoint features research on the connection between climate change and economic instability around the world. Kenney showcases the impact that the United States' current administration has on its position as leaders in climate efforts. Additionally, the viewpoint showcases the cost, both human and financial, in damage caused by climate change and its connection to peoples' access to food in impacted countries.

The 2016 U.S. presidential election gave rise to concerns about how the next administration might—or might not—approach the challenges posed by climate change. Unfortunately, thus far, the current administration has not only ignored these challenges but also has taken steps to undermine efforts to combat them, such as announcing the U.S. intention to withdraw from the landmark Paris Agreement, rescinding the Clean Power Plan, and revoking former President Barack Obama's Memorandum on Climate Change and National Security. Presenting one small sliver of hope at this year's Conference of the Parties, acting Assistant Secretary

"How Climate Change and Water and Food Insecurity Drive Instability," by Carolyn Kenney, Center for American Progress, November 30, 2017. Reprinted by permission.

for the Bureau of Oceans and International Environmental and Scientific Affairs in the U.S. Department of State Judith Garber noted that though "the United States intends to withdraw [from the Paris Agreement] at the earliest opportunity, we remain open to the possibility of rejoining at a later date under terms more favorable to the American people." However, the overall picture remains bleak.

The steps back from climate mitigation and response could not come at a worse time, given the rapidly accumulating costs of a changing global climate. As detailed in a previous Center for American Progress report, since 2011, the United States has experienced 84 extreme weather events, which have resulted in some 2,000 deaths and cost a total of roughly $675 billion in damages. Additionally, according to the most recent Global Climate Risk Index, between 1997 and 2016, "more than 524,000 people died as a direct result of more than 11,000 extreme weather events" around the world, which cost about $3.16 trillion in purchasing power parities. These costs, however, are not distributed evenly around the world; they disproportionately fall on the most vulnerable and least equipped to adapt and rebuild. For instance, as the Planetary Security Initiative calculates, from 2004 to 2014, 58 percent of disaster deaths occurred in countries considered to be ranked among the top 30 most fragile states on the Fragile States Index.

Despite the high costs of extreme weather events, investments aimed at reducing the risks posed by climate change abroad have been insufficient. As pointed out in a report by the U.N. High-Level Panel on Humanitarian Financing, for every $100 spent on development aid projects, "just 40 cents has gone into protecting countries from succumbing to natural disasters." Driving the need for investment further, the report notes that "12 out of a group of 23 low-income countries received less than US$ 10 million for DRR [Disaster Risk Reduction] over 20 years while receiving US$ 5.6 billion in disaster response."

This administration has compounded this problem by moving to slash spending on international and domestic institutions and mechanisms that actively work to prevent costly climate and humanitarian crises. However, it is clear that investing in preventive measures, whether they are aimed at conflict prevention or climate change resilience and mitigation, actually reduces costs in the long run. This is true monetarily and, more importantly, in terms of the cost to human lives and livelihoods. The United States should be making strategic investments to build resilience and allay costly future emergency responses—not cutting the already paltry investments in prevention.

In addition to these direct costs, there are also much higher indirect costs associated with climate-induced disasters, especially in fragile states. Climate change acts as a threat multiplier: Weather shocks and their resulting effects can create and exacerbate political, economic, and social tensions—potentially contributing to cycles of poverty, violence, and migration. As pointed out in a previous CAP report, Syria starkly demonstrates this risk. A prolonged drought linked to climate change devastated farming and herding communities in key agricultural regions, leading hundreds of thousands of rural Syrians to move to the cities. While the Syrian war's causes are complex, the dislocation caused by the drought—and the Syrian government's poor response to the crisis—exacerbated social, economic, and political tensions in rural areas and the cities to which many rural families migrated. This discontent underpinned the initial protests and shaped the conditions that led to the outbreak of conflict in 2011 and the resulting refugee crisis. To date, an estimated 465,000 Syrians have been killed and more than 5.3 million Syrians have been displaced.

Ignoring climate change and its effects will take an increasing toll on human lives and livelihoods, economic prosperity, and peace and security. To demonstrate these losses and the real security risks climate change can pose, this issue brief examines the nexus of climate change, water security, and food security in fragile states and highlights some of the threats to international peace and stability that can emerge—specifically, how these issues can drive instability, as well as how water and food are used during conflict as tools for recruitment and weapons of war.

State of Water and Food Security in the World

The most pressing area of concern at the nexus of climate change and national security is water security. As detailed by the World Bank, the effects of climate change have come and will continue to come through the water cycle; droughts, variable or unpredictable rainfall for agriculture or herding, pollution and contamination, and floods or extreme weather can have devastating impacts. The scarcity or surfeit of water can reverberate through crucial systems, affecting food production, pricing, and availability; energy production; transportation and supply chains; densely populated urban areas; and basic environmental systems. These effects will become more severe as populations, cities, and economies continue to grow and strain increasingly limited water resources. The World Bank estimates that roughly 1.6 billion people already live in countries with water scarcity, and that number could double in just two decades.

Directly related to water security is the issue of food security. According to the Food and Agriculture Organization of the United Nations and others, global hunger increased in 2016 following a long decline, affecting 815 million people worldwide, compared with 777 million in 2015. The deterioration of food security was particularly intense in areas experiencing conflict, most notably when compounded by extreme weather events affecting water supplies. Indeed, famine and/or crisis-level food insecurity situations were present in four countries undergoing conflict this year: South Sudan; Nigeria; Somalia; and Yemen.

Climate Change, Water, and Food Supplies as Drivers of Instability

The overlapping incidence of water and food insecurity and conflict is no coincidence; these trends interact with and contribute to one another. The impacts of water and food scarcity can undermine basic livelihoods and exacerbate social tensions, which can lead to instability and conflict if left unaddressed or when compounded by other social or political grievances. The consequences of these intersecting challenges vary greatly around the world as a result of a number of factors, such as political, social, and economic conditions; existing infrastructure; and policy decisions.

For instance, as water and food supplies become constrained, often as a result of extreme weather events spurred by climate change, social tensions over access to available resources can escalate and even turn violent. This is especially dangerous in fragile states that have a history of conflict and in areas where access to these resources has been politicized. The United Nations has found that while disputes over natural resources are rarely the sole driver of violent conflict, they certainly can be a contributing factor when other drivers are present, such as poverty, ethnic polarization, and poor governance. Examples of such disputes can be found all over the world, including in Sudan, Syria, and Yemen, among others.

Water and Food Supplies as Recruitment Tools During Conflict

In the lead-up to and following the eruption of conflicts, resources such as water and food, especially when they are constrained, are often also used as tools for manipulation and recruitment into violent groups. For instance, a recent *National Geographic* investigation, based on more than 100 interviews with farmers and agricultural officials over three years, concluded that poor government policies and climate-exacerbated drought across rural areas of Iraq and Syria made "many of the most environmentally damaged Sunni Arab villages … some of the deep-pocketed jihadists' foremost recruiting grounds" for the Islamic State (IS). The report details that with each extreme weather event and harvest loss, recruiters would appear to distribute gifts, such as food or cash, eventually gaining returns on their investments. For instance, near Tikrit, IS gained "much more support from water-deprived communities than from their better-resourced peers." While likely not the sole reason many in these communities joined the ranks of IS, the effects of water and food scarcity and the targeted presentation of alternatives by recruiters seems to have contributed to some decisions to join in these communities.

Water and Food Supplies as Weapons of War

In addition to being used as a recruitment tool, resources such as water and food can be weaponized by armed parties as a way to exert power and exact outcomes over other armed groups and/or civilian populations. For example, U.N. sanctions monitors recently reported to the U.N. Security Council that South Sudan President Salva Kiir and his government "deliberately prevented life-saving food assistance from reaching some citizens." Such actions were described as "amount[ing] to using food as a weapon of war with the intent to inflict suffering on civilians the government views as opponents to its agenda."

Additionally, in Yemen, where almost 7 million are facing famine and 17 million are completely dependent on humanitarian aid, Saudi Arabia implemented a full blockade on all land, air, and sea ports, effectively cutting off critical humanitarian assistance. While the blockade has been partially lifted on ports controlled by Saudi Arabia's allies, humanitarian access is still being blocked in some areas to devastating effect. In addition to the active conflict, what makes the situation in Yemen particularly disastrous is that according to estimates from 2015, the country has the highest level of water scarcity in the world, with at least 50 percent of the population struggling daily to locate or purchase enough safe water to drink or grow their own food.

US and International Community Responses

While it does not appear that the current U.S. administration will do much to address climate change and the threats it poses, the U.S. nonfederal climate movement has flourished. To date, nonfederal climate initiatives and coalitions—which have proliferated in the wake of the Paris Agreement withdrawal announcement—have largely focused on domestic emissions reduction efforts. But city, state, and private sector actors are beginning to recognize that international climate finance and cooperation are essential if they are to take up the mantle of U.S. climate leadership. This was evident in the unprecedented presence of U.S. nonfederal leaders during the 2017 U.N. climate summit in Bonn, Germany. If these nascent nonfederal climate initiatives—such as the U.S. Climate Alliance, for example, which represents nearly 40 percent of the U.S. economy—realize their latent diplomatic power, they could help keep water and food security on the global agenda.

Additionally, as a result of previous legislation, certain U.S. agencies have provided strategy documents on issues related to food and water security, which can provide ready-made blueprints for action when the political will returns at the federal level. Specifically, as mandated by the Senator Paul Simon Water for the World Act of 2014, the U.S. Agency for International Development and the State Department released a Global Water Strategy to the public on November 15, 2017. The strategic objectives listed in the report include the following:

- Increasing sustainable access to safe drinking water and sanitation services, and the adoption of key hygiene behaviors;
- Encouraging the sound management and protection of freshwater resources;
- Promoting cooperation on shared waters; and,
- Strengthening water-sector governance, financing, and institutions.

And while the strategy did not explicitly discuss how climate change will affect water—and by extension, food security—the release of this strategy is an important step forward and will hopefully be fully implemented in the years to come.

International fora for addressing these concerns include the United Nations, the World Bank, both the G-7 and the G-20, and regional bodies such as the European and African Unions. Each of these bodies, through various formats, concluded that climate change poses both direct and indirect threats to human lives and livelihoods, the environment, economic prosperity, and international peace and security. As such, they have taken steps to try to combat climate change—through the signing of the historic Paris Agreement, the U.N. Sustainable Development Agenda, and initiatives such as the G-7's report and platform on climate and fragility risks and the G-20's Agricultural Market Information System (AMIS). However, more work will be needed in the future, especially absent U.S. federal leadership.

Conclusion

For conflict-prone countries, particularly those most affected by climate change, it is critical to understand how strains on water and food supplies can overlap to drive instability and conflict. Climate impacts can disrupt livelihoods, contribute to decisions to migrate, and exacerbate social tensions. Access to scarce food and water supplies can also be used as a recruitment tool by violent groups, and even harnessed as a weapon of war. If individuals continue to ignore climate change and its impacts, such as those on critical water and food supplies, the consequences will only grow more dire. In a global environment of increasing uncertainty, it is essential to not only change behaviors that perpetuate climate change but also work to build more resilience to and mitigate the inevitable impacts the world will face as a result.

10

World Hunger Is Increasing

Leah Samberg

Leah Samberg is currently a scientist for global programs with the Rainforest Alliance. Her research addresses the interaction of social and environmental processes in small-scale agricultural landscapes and trade-offs between food security and conservation.

In the following viewpoint, Leah Samberg details the increase in world hunger in 2016. The 815 million people who went hungry—11 percent of the world's population—mark the first increase in more than fifteen years. Samberg explains how both conflict and climate change have made significant negative impacts to rural livelihoods—especially emphasizing how war harms farmers. Displacement also leads to more strain on other resources, and may even deplete local resources to feed vulnerable, displaced populations. Samberg's viewpoint also details how to reduce world hunger in the long term, focusing on how rural populations need sustainable ways to support themselves, especially in times of crisis.

A round the globe, about 815 million people—11 percent of the world's population—went hungry in 2016, according to the latest data from the United Nations. This was the first increase in more than 15 years.

Between 1990 and 2015, due largely to a set of sweeping initiatives by the global community, the proportion of undernourished people in the world was cut in half. In 2015, U.N. member countries adopted the Sustainable Development Goals, which doubled down on this success by setting out to end hunger entirely by 2030. But a recent U.N. report shows that, after years of decline, hunger is on the rise again.

As evidenced by nonstop news coverage of floods, fires, refugees and violence, our planet has become a more unstable and less predictable place over the past few years. As these disasters compete for our attention, they make it harder for people in poor, marginalized and war-torn regions to access adequate food.

I study decisions that smallholder farmers and pastoralists, or livestock herders, make about their crops, animals and land. These choices are limited by lack of access to services, markets or credit; by poor governance or inappropriate policies; and by ethnic, gender and educational barriers. As a result, there is often little they can do to maintain secure or sustainable food production in the face of crises.

The new U.N. report shows that to reduce and ultimately eliminate hunger, simply making agriculture more productive will not be enough. It also is essential to increase the options available to rural populations in an uncertain world.

Conflict and Climate Change
Threaten Rural Livelihoods

Around the world, social and political instability are on the rise. Since 2010, state-based conflict has increased by 60 percent and armed conflict within countries has increased by 125 percent. More than half of the food-insecure people identified in the U.N. report (489 million out of 815 million) live in countries with ongoing violence. More than three-quarters of the world's chronically malnourished children (122 million of 155 million) live in conflict-affected regions.

At the same time, these regions are experiencing increasingly powerful storms, more frequent and persistent drought and more variable rainfall associated with global climate change. These trends are not unrelated. Conflict-torn communities are more vulnerable to climate-related disasters, and crop or livestock failure due to climate can contribute to social unrest.

War hits farmers especially hard. Conflict can evict them from their land, destroy crops and livestock, prevent them from acquiring seed and fertilizer or selling their produce, restrict their access to water and forage, and disrupt planting or harvest cycles. Many conflicts play out in rural areas characterized by smallholder agriculture or pastoralism. These small-scale farmers are some of the most vulnerable people on the planet. Supporting them is one of the U.N.'s key strategies for reaching its food security targets.

Disrupted and Displaced

Without other options to feed themselves, farmers and pastoralists in crisis may be forced to leave their land and communities. Migration is one of the most visible coping mechanisms for rural populations who face conflict or climate-related disasters.

Globally, the number of refugees and internally displaced persons doubled between 2007 and 2016. Of the estimated 64 million people who are currently displaced, more than 15 million are linked to one of the world's most severe conflict-related food crises in Syria, Yemen, Iraq, South Sudan, Nigeria and Somalia.

While migrating is uncertain and difficult, those with the fewest resources may not even have that option. New research by my colleagues at the University of Minnesota shows that the most vulnerable populations may be "trapped" in place, without the resources to migrate.

Displacement due to climate disasters also feeds conflict. Drought-induced migration in Syria, for example, has been linked to the conflict there, and many militants in Nigeria have been identified as farmers displaced by drought.

Supporting Rural Communities

To reduce world hunger in the long term, rural populations need sustainable ways to support themselves in the face of crisis. This means investing in strategies to support rural livelihoods that are resilient, diverse and interconnected.

Many large-scale food security initiatives supply farmers with improved crop and livestock varieties, plus fertilizer and other necessary inputs. This approach is crucial, but can lead farmers to focus most or all of their resources on growing more productive maize, wheat or rice. Specializing in this way increases risk. If farmers cannot plant seed on time or obtain fertilizers, or if rains fail, they have little to fall back on.

Increasingly, agricultural research and development agencies, NGOs and aid programs are working to help farmers maintain traditionally diverse farms by providing financial, agronomic and policy support for production and marketing of native crop and livestock species. Growing many different locally adapted crops provides for a range of nutritional needs and reduces farmers' risk from variability in weather, inputs or timing.

While investing in agriculture is viewed as the way forward in many developing regions, equally important is the ability of farmers to diversify their livelihood strategies beyond the farm. Income from off-farm employment can buffer farmers against crop failure or livestock loss, and is a key component of food security for many agricultural households.

Training, education, and literacy programs allow rural people to access a greater range of income and information sources. This is especially true for women, who are often more vulnerable to food insecurity than men.

Conflict also tears apart rural communities, breaking down traditional social structures. These networks and relationships facilitate exchanges of information, goods and services, help protect natural resources, and provide insurance and buffering mechanisms.

In many places, one of the best ways to bolster food security is by helping farmers connect to both traditional and innovative social networks, through which they can pool resources, store food, seed and inputs and make investments. Mobile phones enable farmers to get information on weather and market prices, work cooperatively with other producers and buyers and obtain aid, agricultural extension or veterinary services. Leveraging multiple forms of connectivity is a central strategy for supporting resilient livelihoods.

In the past two decades the world has come together to fight hunger. This effort has produced innovations in agriculture, technology and knowledge transfer. Now, however, the compounding crises of violent conflict and a changing climate show that this approach is not enough. In the planet's most vulnerable places, food security depends not just on making agriculture more productive, but also on making rural livelihoods diverse, interconnected and adaptable.

11

The Import Impact on Food Security

Lanessa Cago

Lanessa Cago is a contributor for World Atlas, *which aims to provide informative content surrounding on the topic of geography.*

In the following viewpoint, Lanessa Cago details the impact countries have on one another regarding food imports. With international populations continuing to grow, the United States, China, Germany, Japan, and the United Kingdom have become the countries that import the most food to other economies. The viewpoint also explains that by the year 2050 it's estimated that more than half of the world's population will be reliant on food sourced from other countries. Countries that are currently unable to produce their own food include Afghanistan, Burkina Faso, Burundi, Cameroon, and more.

F ood security was, and still is, a major issue, for both wealthy and poverty-ridden countries all over the world. This should come as no surprise with the ever present inflation of food demand that stems in large from a continually rising global population. According to the United Nations Food and Agricultural Organization, in 2011 food prices rose for eight straight months, which made the already unpredictable situation in global food markets worse than ever. Such increases may have been beneficial for some countries, especially those who were the top exporters. For the rest of the world, however, such a phenomenon meant real trouble, such as economic crises, major social unrest, and even the decline of certain governments' powers.

One in Six People in the World Rely on Imports to Feed Them Today

Continued population and/or income increase have pushed the United States, China, Germany, Japan and the United Kingdom up the list of the Countries Who Import the Most Food. According to the Standard International Trade Classification, or SITC, food are the commodities that fall under sections 0, 1 and 4 as well as division 22. Section 0 is comprised of food and live animals, section 1 of beverages and tobacco and section 4 of vegetable and animal fats and oils. Division 22, on the other hand, includes oil kernels, oil nuts and oil seeds.

The United States, being one of the world's largest economies, imports a total of $133 billion USD worth of food and food products, followed by China at $105.26 billion USD, Germany at $98.90 billion USD, Japan at $68.86 billion USD, the United Kingdom at $66.54 billion USD, the Netherlands at $64.38 billion USD, France at $62.29 billion USD, Italy at $51.34 billion USD, Belgium at $40.87 billion USD, and the Russian Federation at $38.60 billion USD.

However, importing a high amount of food does not necessarily mean that a country is food insecure. In fact, many of the world's largest food importing countries also happen to be among the world's wealthiest. It is important to note that majority of the countries importing the most food in the world have the potential to become completely food sufficient if they choose to do so. In theses cases, where food insecurity is not of concern, food is imported to create more variety for the consumer, not to prevent starvation within the population. Importing a large amount of food does not mean that a country is food insecure.

Which Countries in the World Are Food Insecure?

When food is imported out of a necessity for sustenance, countries become dependent on outside sources as a way of feeding their populations. This is when food insecurity occurs. Currently, there are at least 34 countries who are unable to produce their own food due to water and land limitations, which represents a large portion of the global population who must rely on imported food in order to avoid starvation. These countries are listed below.

Are Countries Becoming More Food Insecure?

By year 2050, more than half of the world's population is expected to rely in food sourced from other countries. A comprehensive study conducted by Marianela Fader of Potsdam Institute for Climate Impact Research shows that population pressures will push many nations to make maximizing their domestic food production capacity a top priority. This conclusion was made after the research team computed the growing capability of each and every country to do so, and differentiated their respective production capacities with their current and future food requirements. The team's model made use of soil categories, climate information, and patterns of land utilization for each country, which were then translated into yields for numerous kinds of crops. By using the information on hand regarding the respective populations and water and food intakes of each nation, the team was able to closely evaluate what percentage of its food requirement each country could produce on their own in the future.

Significant issues with food security will continue to trouble the world in coming years if the aforementioned study plays out to be an accurate projection. One way to combat such concern is for each country, rich or poor, to focus its resources on improving their agricultural productivity, which can play an important role in alleviating food shortages. Another possible solution is diet modifications geared towards the consumption of crops that are already produced locally, although further studies will have to be conducted to determine the viability of this option.

What Countries Import the Most Food?

The United States, being one of the world's largest economies, imports a total of $133 billion USD worth of food and food products, followed by China at $105.26 billion USD, Germany at $98.90 billion USD, Japan at $68.86 billion USD, and the United Kingdom at $66.54 billion USD.

Countries Who Are Unable to Produce Their Own Food

1. Afghanistan
2. Burkina Faso
3. Burundi
4. Cameroon
5. Central African Republic
6. Chad
7. Democratic Republic of the Congo
8. Djibouti
9. Eritrea
10. Ethiopia
11. Guinea
12. Iraq
13. Kenya
14. Lesotho
15. Liberia
16. Madagascar
17. Malawi
18. Mali
19. Mauritania
20. Mozambique
21. Myanmar
22. Nepal
23. Niger

24. North Korea
25. Republic of the Congo
26. Sierra Leone
27. Somalia
28. South Sudan
29. Sudan
30. Swaziland
31. Syria
32. Uganda
33. Yemen
34. Zimbabwe

12

East Africa's Food Crisis

Audrey Dorelien

Audrey Dorelien is an assistant professor at the Humphrey School of Public Affairs and a faculty affiliate of the Minnesota Population Center at the University of Minnesota.

The following viewpoint details what has caused the sharp increase in food prices in East Africa, including the effect of an increasing population on food demand. With some of the poorest countries in the world being located in East Africa, drought, dependence on rain-fed agriculture, low agricultural productivity, and frequent conflict make it all the more difficult to grow food consistently. The viewpoint also shows how the growing middle classes in China and India also have an impact on economic growth in African countries.

T he prices of agricultural commodities, including staples of many African diets, have risen sharply over the last several years. The sharpest rises have been within the past six months. Since 2005, the prices of maize and wheat have doubled, and the price of rice has now reached unprecedented levels (see Table 1). According to the World Bank, the Food and Agricultural Organization of the United Nations, and the United States Department of Agriculture, rising prices are likely to persist through 2015.

The factors leading to increased prices and the resultant food crisis are diverse and complex. Most factors, however, can be thought of as having impacts on the supply of food and/or the demand for food. The supply of food may be affected by land and water constraints, underinvestment in rural infrastructure and agriculture, lack of access to fertilizer and irrigation, trade policies, and weather disruptions. Factors that affect the demand for food include rising energy prices and conversion of croplands to biofuel production, population growth, globalization of food markets, and changing diets. The current food crisis is, in the simplest terms, a result of rapid growth in food demand in conjunction with a decline in the growth of food supply.

A number of recent reports have implicated population growth as one of the main contributors to increasing food demand. There has not, however, been a comprehensive examination of how population factors (size, growth, distribution, and composition) may affect both the supply and demand for staple food. This article will explore select aspects of the population-food crisis relationship, including several that are not typically discussed, and provide examples from East Africa, which has been particularly hard-hit by the food crisis.

East Africa and Food Security

East Africa, which includes Burundi, Eritrea, Ethiopia, Kenya, Rwanda, Somalia, Tanzania, and Uganda, imports fertilizers and food and contains some of the poorest countries in the world. Periodic drought, dependence on rain-fed agriculture, low agricultural productivity, and frequent conflict undermine local food production, contribute to food insecurity, and create greater dependence on food aid. For example, the December 2007 post-election conflict in Kenya disrupted production and trade and displaced farmers and laborers, which caused the normally food-secure regions of Central and Western Kenya to become food insecure. The conflict resulted in a post-harvest loss of 300,000 metric tons of maize. While East Africa is not as dependent on food imports (such as rice) as West Africa, this combination of factors makes most countries in East Africa especially vulnerable

Table 1: Agricultural Commodity Prices ($US/metric ton),
2005 to the Second Quarter, 2008

CEREALS	2005	2006	2007	1ST QUARTER 2008	2ND QUARTER 2008
Wheat	152	192	255	411	347
Maize	98	122	163	220	259
Rice	288	304	332	516	953

Source: International Monetary Fund (IMF), "Table 3. Actual Market Prices for Non-Fuel and Fuel Commodities, 2005-2008," IMF Primary Commodities Prices (www.imf.org, accessed Aug. 12, 2008).

to higher global food prices. Recent research in nine developing countries found that higher prices of staple food commodities were associated with a significant increase in poverty. This increasing poverty and food security have led to an immediate need for food aid in several East African countries. Unfortunately, however, food aid volumes are near a 50-year low and the higher food prices mean that money dedicated to food aid simply doesn't provide as much food as in the past.

One might expect higher food prices to benefit rural farmers and lead to higher incomes and increased production, but in East Africa this isn't necessarily the case. It is difficult for small farmers to increase production in response to higher prices for several reasons, including: lack of available land, inadequate irrigation, rising fertilizer prices, inability to get insurance and loans, and reluctance to risk investment with no guaranteed return. In fact, despite the higher prices of the foods they are producing, farmers in some parts of East Africa have actually planted less this year.

In recent history, East Africa has been one of the most food-insecure regions in the world. Food security, which is defined as "when all people at all times have both physical and economic access to sufficient food to meet their dietary needs for a productive and healthy life," is a broad and complex measure. It is usually studied through three dimensions: food availability, food access, and biological utilization/absorption of food. For East Africa's poor, who typically spend 50 percent to 70 percent of their budgets on food, higher food prices lead to reduced food consumption as well as a less nutritious diet Projections from the Famine Early Warning Systems Network (FEWS-NET) indicate that the severity of food insecurity will increase in parts of East Africa, especially Somalia, eastern Ethiopia, and northern Kenya, in the third quarter of 2008.

Population and Current Food Crisis

The majority of recent reports on the food crisis focus principally on population growth and an increasing demand for food. Population growth, however, is one of several demographic factors likely contributing to the current food crisis. Urbanization, the growth of the middle class and associated changes in consumption patterns, migration and wage employment, large family size, and HIV/AIDS are all contributing factors as well.

Population growth has been the most discussed demographic dimension of the food crisis because of its very direct impact on the growth in food demand. Last year the world population grew by 1.2 percent and it is expected to reach 7 billion in 2012 and 9.3 billion in 2050. Demand for food is projected to double by 2030 and 20 percent of that increase is attributed to population growth. Neither population growth nor food production are evenly distributed across the globe. For example, the total fertility rate (TFR), a measure of the average number of children a woman will have over her lifetime, in East Africa in 2007 was 5.5 compared to the world average of 2.7 (see Table 2). Rural fertility is particularly high and stagnant in most countries, such as Uganda, Burundi, and Ethiopia, and when combined with lowering mortality, is resulting in rapid population growth. The current East African population of approximately 300 million is projected to increase to 438 million by 2025 and to 650 million by 2050.

In the past, technological improvements in agriculture allowed food production to comfortably exceed population growth, resulting in declining food prices. This pattern of declining food prices, however, has recently reversed and there is growing concern among policymakers and researchers as to whether the previous progress will continue.

The relationship between population growth and food security is not limited to increased demand for food. Population growth can also have an impact on the food supply and access. In many areas population growth has been associated with land fragmentation and resettlement schemes in fragile environments that directly affect food production. Specifically, land fragmentation contributes to inefficient and destructive farming practices and increased cultivation of marginal land, which often reduces food production. Because of population growth and land distribution policies, the average farm size in Ethiopia fell from 1.2 hectares to 0.8 hectares during the 1990s.

Migration for Wage Opportunities

In many countries a large share of rural income is earned by rural residents who migrate temporarily to places where they can find jobs. Research in East Africa has shown that rural households are increasingly dependent on wage labor not only as a coping strategy during hunger seasons, but also as a routine livelihood strategy to meet their food needs. In Kenya, wage labor now accounts for more than 50 percent of rural households' income. The diversification of rural income is generally driven by social, cultural, and economic change, but population pressure and land fragmentation also play a role. As landholdings become too small to support households, and with excess family labor available, adolescent and young adult family members often migrate to supplement their farming livelihood with wage employment.

This increased dependence on wage employment may have mixed effects on food security. First, households may suffer from rising staple food prices if employment opportunities are reduced by energy, fertilizer, transportation costs, and the inability of employers to secure loans. Second, household food production

Table 2: 2008 Population, Total Fertility Rates, and Projected 2025 Population in East African Countries

	2008 POPULATION (MILLIONS)	TOTAL FERTILITY RATE (TFR)	2025 PROJECTED POPULATION (MILLIONS)
World	6,705	2.7	8,000
East Africa	301	5.4	440
Ethiopia	79.1	5.3	110.5
Tanzania	40.2	5.3	58.2
Kenya	38.0	4.9	51.3
Uganda	29.2	6.7	56.4
Rwanda	9.6	6.0	14.6
Somalia	9.0	6.7	14.3
Burundi	8.9	6.8	15.0
Eritrea	5.0	5.3	7.7

Note: Regional total includes other East African countries. The total fertility rate measures the average number of lifetime births a woman would have given current birth rates.

Source: Carl Haub and Mary Mederios Kent, 2008 World Population Data Sheet.

may decrease as adults migrate for employment and education opportunities and spend less time laboring on the farm. Finally, wage employment may actually improve food security in regions where household farming yields vary greatly from year to year and are highly vulnerable to drought. For these households, wage employment may serve as a risk mitigation strategy against crop failures.

The Growing Middle Class and Changes in Consumption

Media reports have also focused on the growing incomes of households in China and India, which account for almost 40 percent of the world's population, and have had strong economic growth rates. Based on this trend, the world's middle class will grow substantially. The World Bank estimated that by 2030 "fully 1.2 billion people in developing countries—15 percent of the world population—will belong to the global middle class, up from 400 million in 2005."

Rising incomes are often accompanied by changing food preferences. There is a greater emphasis on the consumption of meats, fruits, and vegetables and a move away from traditional staples. Thus, global trends are characterized by not only a growing demand for more food but also for different types of food. The growing demand for meat leads to a disproportionate increase in demand for grain and protein feed needed to produce meat. Producing one pound of beef requires seven pounds of corn feed.

The growth of the middle class and economic growth in developing countries have also increased global energy demand. Rising petroleum use in developing countries has contributed to rising oil prices, which have affected food production in two ways. First, rising fuel prices have increased the cost of fertilizers, fuel, and pesticides used in agriculture. This has caused the prices of agricultural products to increase, and in certain places caused output to decrease. Second, the rising oil prices have increased the demand and production of biofuels as substitutes for oil. The increased demand for and production of corn, which is converted to ethanol, has diverted croplands away from food production and has contributed directly to the rising prices of corn and other staples.

Urbanization and Its Effect on Food Demand and Supply

The world is becoming increasingly urban, and by the end of 2008, more than half of the world's population will be living in urban areas. Future population growth is expected to occur almost exclusively in urban areas. By 2030, the world's urban population is expected to reach 4.9 billion, while the rural population is expected to decrease by 28 million. Furthermore, the pace of urbanization will grow the fastest in regions that currently have low levels of urbanization, such as in East Africa. Consequently, these regions will have a growing nonagricultural population that relies on purchased food and is susceptible to increases in food prices. In Mozambique, for example, urban residents purchase 83 percent of their food, while rural residents purchase only 30 percent.

Urbanization, like income growth, is associated with increased consumption of meats, fruits, and vegetables. In East Africa, while the middle classes are growing in cities like Nairobi and Addis Ababa, there is little evidence so far that the urban poor, who are the majority, are changing their food preferences to the higher-priced products.

Urbanization is also often associated with decreases in food supply due to a loss of agricultural land and dietary diversification. The expansion of urban space tends to affect farm lands because many cities and towns are located in rich agricultural lands. A compounding factor is that urban growth is increasingly land-intensive. Urban space grows faster than urban populations, evident as urban sprawl. Cities and their growing populations also increasingly compete with the agricultural sector for scarce water resources, resulting in less water for irrigation. For example, in Tanzania, rapidly growing demand for water for domestic and industrial activities in the towns of Arusha and Moshi has led to the damming of large rivers to ensure urban water supply. Decreases in the water available for agriculture will further inhibit the ability of farmers to increase food production.

HIV/AIDS

The spread of HIV/AIDS is also undermining food security in sub-Saharan Africa, including the East African countries of Kenya, Tanzania, and Uganda. HIV/AIDS reduces agriculture production through a number of factors, creating both immediate and cumulative impacts. HIV/AIDS affects people in their prime working ages, 15 to 49; in Kenya, Uganda, and Tanzania, more than 5 percent of the working-age population is infected. Furthermore, subsistence agriculture relies heavily on human labor, particularly women's labor. Therefore, in regions with high HIV/AIDS prevalence like southern Africa, where subsistence agriculture is the norm, HIV/AIDS-related illness and deaths reduce the agricultural labor force, resulting in less land being farmed, reduced yields, and less intensive crops being grown. In Kenya, a study found that the death of an adult female household member resulted in fewer grain crops grown, while the death of an adult male resulted in decreased production of cash crops such as sugar and coffee.

HIV/AIDS may also exacerbate poverty. Household income may fall if the infected individual was a wage earner, and expenses may increase because of new health care costs. The redistribution of money for medicine and funeral expenses by afflicted households reduces the income available for food and investments to improve agricultural production. Food production is also threatened by the loss of agricultural knowledge when infected individuals die. The food crisis is also likely to exacerbate the impact of HIV/AIDS as infected individuals, who have heightened nutritional needs, find it more difficult to purchase foods.

Conclusion

Several population factors play an important role in the increasing and changing nature of the demand for food, while also constricting supply and access to food. Population's role is often neither direct nor simple, and its impacts can vary at the local and global level. Nonetheless, many demographic trends that affect food supply and demand, especially rapid population growth, urbanization, population density of the rural poor, and migration for employment, are projected to continue. In the absence of significant policy reforms and technological change, these demographic factors will likely continue to affect food security in coming decades. East Africa in particular is likely to face many population-related food security challenges. Policies aimed at the current food crisis or at achieving the United Nations' Millennium Development Goal on hunger—by 2015, to reduce by half the proportion of people who suffer from hunger—must not ignore the complex role of population.

13

The Price of a Healthy Diet

Laura Donnelly

Laura Donnelly is the health editor of the Telegraph, *an award-winning multimedia news brand based in the United Kingdom.*

In the following viewpoint, Laura Donnelly details just how expensive it is to eat healthily—three times more than consuming unhealthy food, to be exact. With references to studies by Cambridge University, Donnelly showcases that 1,000 calories of healthy items cost an average of £7.49 in 2012 (about $12.00 USD), compared to 1,000 calories of unhealthy items costing just £2.50 (about $4.00 USD). Donnelly posits that the increase in price difference also has a significant impact on food security in the United Kingdom.

Eating healthily costs three times as much as consuming unhealthy food—and the price gap is widening, according to a study by Cambridge University.

Researchers examined almost 100 popular items of food, which is defined under Government criteria as healthy or not.

They found that 1,000 calories made up from healthy items, such as lean salmon, yoghurts and tomatoes, cost an average of £7.49 in 2012.

The same calorie intake from less healthy items, such as pizza, beef burgers, and doughnuts, could be purchased for an average of £2.50.

The gap between the two 1,000 calorie baskets is now £4.99, the research found, when ten years ago it was £3.88.

The average increase of healthy foods rose by £1.84 per 1,000 calories over the decade, while unhealthy food rose by 73 pence for the same energy intake, the study found.

Researchers from the University's Centre for Diet and Activity Research, called on Government to do more to bring down the costs of healthy food.

Lead author Nicholas Jones said: "Food poverty and the rise of food banks have recently been an issue of public concern in the UK, but as well as making sure people don't go hungry it is also important that a healthy diet is affordable."

"The increase in the price difference between more and less healthy foods is a factor that may contribute towards growing food insecurity, increasing health inequalities, and a deterioration in the health of the population."

Researchers tracked the price of 94 key food and drink items from 2002 to 2012.

They found that more healthy foods were consistently more expensive than less healthy foods, with absolute costs increasing more than those of unhealthy fare.

In 2002, 1,000 kcal of healthy food—as defined by government criteria—cost an average of £5.65, compared to purchasing the same quantity of energy from less healthy food at £1.77.

By 2012 this cost had changed to £7.49 for more healthy and £2.50 for less healthy foods.

While less healthy foods had a slightly greater price rise in percentage terms, the absolute increase was significantly more for more healthy foods—a total average increase of £1.84 per 1,000 kcal for more healthy food across the decade, compared 73 pence for less healthy food.

The cost of diet-related ill health to the National Health Service has been estimated to be £5.8 billion annually.

Mr Jones said: "The finding shows that there could well be merit in public health bodies monitoring food prices in relation to nutrient content, hopefully taking into account a broader selection of foods than we were able to in this study."

Senior author Pablo Monsivais said Government policies needed to do more to address high prices of healthier foods, and subsidise some healthy foods for those on low incomes.

The food and beverages studied were those which remained in the "basket" used by the Office of National Statistics' Consumer Price Index for the entire 10 years.

Dr John Middleton, from the Faculty of Public Health, said rising prices of healthy foods were pushing too many families towards unhealthy fare and contributing to worrying increases in obesity and diabetes.

"The cost of healthy options is one of many reasons why we have food poverty in the UK," he said. "This is not just about individual choice. Blaming individuals for not knowing how to cook well on a low budget so they don't fill up on cheap junk food won't help."

He called on the government to set up an independent working group to monitor UK nutrition and hunger status. This will give us the independent and authoritative data to fully understand what is happening and what needs to be done to stop the scandal of food poverty.

"When teachers report that school children are arriving at school unable to concentrate because they have not had breakfast, we have to take action to give our children the best start in life," he said.

Healthy Foods 2002 2012 (£/1000kcal):

- Tomatoes £9.53 £13.21
- Vegetable burgers £2.17 £2.80
- Semi-skimmed milk £1.07 £1.73
- Canned tuna £3.22 £5.54
- Yoghurt £14.09 £17.68
- Salmon £4.11 £6.87
- Lean beef mince £2.64 £4.52

- Iceberg lettuce £11.36 £16.45
- Cauliflower £6.89 £9.97

Unhealthy foods 2002 2012 (£/1000kcal):

- Frozen pizza £2.10 £1.58
- Beefburger £1.24 £2.01
- Bacon £3.14 £4.15
- Cola drink £2.61 £4.24
- Doughnut £0.96 £0.98
- Ice cream £1.50 £1.57
- Box of chocolates £6.25 £4.68
- Jar of jam £0.86 £0.99
- Sponge cake £1.26 £1.21
- Fizzy energy drink £4.09 £5.55

Prices are average prices from a range of products, using data from the Office for National Statistics' basket of purchases. Foods are ranked as more healthy or less healthy, using Government criteria.

14

Are GMOs the Key?

Lisa Cornish

Lisa Cornish is a Devex reporter based in Canberra, Australia, where she focuses on the Australian aid community. Lisa formerly worked with News Corp Australia as a data journalist for the national network.

In the following viewpoint, Lisa Cornish details how on an international level food security is one of the greatest developmental challenges. Due to climate change, land that is suitable for food cultivation has changed and has also been impacted by natural disasters like flooding and drought. Not only does the viewpoint go into how GMOs can make a positive impact in the future of food security, it also explains why there is an anti-GMO argument in the first place.

F ood security is, and will continue to be, one of our greatest ongoing development challenges. We not only need to provide food and nutrition for a growing global population, but we must do so in the face of mounting environmental challenges. The global climate is changing, and land suitable for agriculture and food production is changing with it. Salinification and desertification, flooding and drought, and natural disasters threaten agriculture across the globe. With changing temperatures, meanwhile, come new risks from pests and diseases.

"Are GMOs the Key to Global Food Security?" by Lisa Cornish, Devex, January 15, 2018. This article originally appeared in Devex, the media platform for the global development community. Reprinted by permission.

Agricultural and food security experts are investigating a range of ways to address these challenges. Solutions range from everything from new breeding programs, to better monitoring and evaluation, to farming strategies that reduce waste and increase yield.

But in discussing a food-secure future, the role of genetically modified organisms remains a raging debate.

At the core of the anti-GMO argument is the role large corporations play in the development, implementation, and profit from GMO products—largely Monsanto. Organizations such as Monsanto grew as GMO leaders due to the initial costs involved in the research, development, testing, and intellectual property associated with GMO. Monsanto has developed a range of crops that produce higher yield—including the controversial roundup ready crops, which are pesticide resistant. Monsanto not only makes money from selling high yield seed, but all the associated products that need to be sprayed on them to produce the best output.

Opponents raise concern over the environmental impacts of such crops and the patent stipulations for small farmers, and they challenge the science and information coming from organizations such as Monsanto. This concern has led to the cultivation of GMOs being banned or prohibited in more than 30 regions, not including bans that have occurred at subregional levels, as well as food labelling standards identifying products as GMO free.

Today, as technology is becoming more accessible and less expensive, smaller labs and researchers are able to produce GMOs at a reduced costs—with the seed produced available for public good, not profit. And this allows them to respond to small, localized food production issues such as bananas in Uganda and papaya in Hawaii.

For the development sector—where the impact of lost local crops can mean loss of income, increased poverty and loss of culture—does "public good" GMO change the debate?

In this five-part series, we look at various sides of the GMO debate to understand the continuing concerns. And we explore whether the conversation changes when we remove corporation and profit from the debate.

In part one, we investigate the scientific argument which favors GMOs for the purpose of creating a food secure future.

Science and GMOs

Aside from the corporations profiting from GMOs, scientists are one of the most vocal groups in favor of the use of GMOs. In June 2016, 129 Nobel Laureates signed a letter urging Greenpeace to re-examine and abandon their campaign against GMOs. In their letter, they argue that there has never been any evidence of health issues associated with GMOs and the impact on the environment is less harmful than traditional agriculture. They also noted that GMO has the potential to greatly reduce death and disease from issues such as Vitamin A deficiency in developing countries.

Today, scientific research continues to find no health risk from GMOs and scientists are being urged to engage on the debate.

Among those leading the charge are Dr Marina Trigueros and Dr Hugo Alonso who have established GMOonly—an initiative dedicated to the promotion of GMOs and the sale of products made with GMOs. Trigueros, with 10 years of scientific research experience in plant molecular biology, and Alonso, a researcher in plant genetics and physiology, told Devex that their frustration over the negative perceptions of GMO led to their initiative.

"We started with this GMO initiative in early 2017," Alonso said. "We were three scientists, all with experience working with GMO in different stages of research, but found the research was being hampered by policies which were making it difficult to bring GM products to the market. To bring a GM product to market, the approval processes take a very long time and regulations make it extremely expensive. We wanted to be able to do something about it."

Fighting the Negative Press

For Trigueros, the science and the rigorous testing and approval processes GMOs are required to go through before reaching the market should build public confidence—they are put through a tougher process than any other food product. But strong lobbying from organizations against GMOs has created a negative public perspective that even science is having a hard time to break through.

"There has only recently been any lobbying in favor of GMO," Alonso said. "The big problem is that companies or organizations using GMOs are keeping it under the radar. They are concerned that if it goes public, they will receive negative press."

In the past, the negative press companies such as Monsanto have received, Alonso said, were valid. "They have done things they probably shouldn't," he said. "Like trying to control the market. But that was 20 years ago, when they were just beginning in this space." With the changing market and reduced cost of technology, the science has become more accessible and available to assist with the food and health challenges specific to developing countries—not just the market needs of the developed world.

"GM is a technology that can be used in different ways," Alonso said. "If a company has a policy that is negative for farmers, it is not a problem with the GMO—it is a problem with the company."

To promote positive press and encourage governments to open the door to growing GMOs, Trigueros said scientists need to play a critical role—but to date they have been doing a poor job.

"Scientists have not been good at selling, explaining, or educating the public on GMOs," she said. "We can make it boring and too scientific. And that means we haven't been able to create a positive viewpoint."

And this has meant that the concept of "Frankenfoods" continues to be associated with GMOs.

"In Africa, where smallholder farmers have been assisting in the development and testing of GMOs there are still issues," Trigueros said. "Because of the fear generated around the concept of GMOs, the governments are not allowing it to be introduced. They think it is weird technology and just assume the food is bad."

Despite there being strong arguments for GMO to support the needs of the developing world, the perceptions of the developed world dominate—and GMO-free branding on products means consumers are more likely to be educated on why they need to avoid GMOs. It is a difficult education cycle to compete against. Combined with supermarkets full of food, Alonso said it is difficult to explain to consumers in developing countries why creating more food should be an important issue to them.

For scientists, GMOs are not the only solution for food security—but they are an important one. "Combined with improved farming conditions, better use of water and reducing waste, GMOs can help to create better food options," Trigueros said.

And with the changing environment, she has no doubt that the future of food will be GMO.

"In ten years we are not going to have this discussion," Trigueros said. "GMOs are going to be there. People will accept them and we hope to even see organic shops accepting them. The new generations will understand this is the food of science, and they will be fine with that."

Can "Public Good" GMO Change the Conversation?

Despite the confidence of Trigueros that a GMO future is a reality, public debate still needs to change to make it a reality. And the concept of promoting GMO as a public good science, not linked to large corporations, is being tested through film.

The documentary Food Evolution, commissioned by the Institute of Food Technologists and narrated by astrophysicist Neil deGrasse Tyson, has been playing at a range of conferences and events throughout the world to spark discussion and highlight the scientific argument—including at events supported by GMOonly.

The documentary aims to come at the debate from a clean slate, discussing both sides of the argument. It ends heavily in favor of science to promote the social and community benefits in places such as Hawaii and Uganda, while downplaying the role of corporations.

"It is new to us to try and show both sides of the story," Trigueros said. "It is important to understand that for both sides, it comes from the heart—including from science."

At a screening at the Australian National University in Canberra last September, the audience were asked about their perspective on GMOs before the film—displaying a red, orange or green card to say if they were against, undecided or for GMOs. Red and orange dominated.

After the screening they were asked the question again—and a significant number were changed to green. It was a positive sign for Trigueros and Alonso that the public good debate of GMO had legs. They are hoping the film can encourage debate and discussion among a wide and diverse audience.

Globally, scientists—including Nobel Laureate Richard Roberts—are becoming more vocal on the need for GMOs to assist the developing world and will continue to push for greater acceptance of GMOs within programs to support better food security and nutrition.

But science is just one part of the story.

15

Trade Wars and the American Farmer

Knowledge@Wharton High School

Knowledge@Wharton High School, or KWHS, aims to provide high school students and educators around the world with a deeper understanding of business and personal finance and to equip them with the skills to excel in the global marketplace. It is a part of the Wharton School of the University of Pennsylvania, a world leader in business education.

This viewpoint showcases the current economic situation of farmers in the United States and how this impacts food supply and pricing. Some of the issues with the industry are due to improved fertilizer and seeds that have led to a global oversupply of crops, which drives prices down and results in less money for farmers. However, another major factor has been China's decision to raise tariffs (government taxes on import and exports) on $600 billion of US goods in retaliation for President Donald Trump's decision to hike tariffs on $200 billion of Chinese goods.

The John Deere tractor has long been a symbol of farming in the U.S. Its signature bright green and yellow colors are often silhouetted against a grand expanse of field or crop, emerging from dust clouds with motor rumbling and blades spinning.

That's why on May 17 it was most telling when Deere & Co., the farm supply company that makes and sells those tractors, threshers and much more for the agriculture industry, announced

"How the Trade War with China Is Hurting U.S. Farmers," Knowledge@Wharton High School is part of the Wharton Global Youth Program at the Wharton School, University of Pennsylvania. Reprinted by permission.

a cautious financial forecast and dwindling earnings. The company cut earnings and sales growth projections for 2019 and reported second-quarter earnings that came in under estimates for a fifth straight quarter. What's more, it is cutting production by 20% at two of its largest factories. This financial news all points to one thing: U.S. farmers are struggling.

An "Agvocate" for Her Industry

In states like Iowa, Nebraska, Minnesota and Illinois, where the economy depends heavily on the farming business, many farmers can't afford these days to buy new John Deere equipment. *The Morning Brew* business newsletter points to three main reasons for this: technologically improved fertilizer and seeds that have led to a global oversupply of crops, driving prices down and resulting in less money for farmers selling what they produce; bad Midwest weather that delayed planting; and the escalating trade war with China.

This third factor has been dominating recent headlines. Last week, China said it planned to raise tariffs (government taxes on imports and exports) on $60 billion of U.S. goods as retaliation for U.S. President Donald Trump's previous move to hike tariffs on $200 billion of Chinese goods. As each country makes its latest move, the fallout continues, for businesses and the U.S. stock market. Amid trade-war tumult, the Dow Jones Industrial Average plunged more than 600 points in a day, the worst one-day drop since January.

America's Farmers are casualties of this trade war. Prior to the trade war, China and Hong Kong combined were the second-largest export market for U.S. pork. Chinese pork buyers have cancelled thousands of metric tons of U.S. pork orders in the escalating tariff exchange of the last few weeks, eroding the $6.5 billion market for American pork. China is also the No. 1 global buyer of soybeans. Throughout this tariff exchange with the U.S., China has capped U.S. imports of the product. That is to say that the country is limiting shipments of soybeans into its markets from the U.S.

In a recent opinion piece, Davie Stephens, president of the American Soybean Association, said, "Trade is the lifeblood of the

U.S. soybean industry, and right now it is ebbing away as soybean growers are unduly caught in the crossfire of the U.S.-China trade war…the effects of the prolonged trade war have already caused soybean prices to fall to levels at which any sale only locks in a loss." Millions of Chinese consumers, who once bought about 60% of American agriculture exports, have stopped buying their products. Added Stephens: "As we plant our 2019 crop, unsold soybean supplies are expected to double before harvest begins in September, further depressing prices and forcing older farmers to consider retiring early to protect their equity and younger ones to look for other careers."

Makenna Green, 18, says she is not going anywhere. As the sixth generation to grow up and live on her family's row crop farm in East Central Illinois, the recent Arthur Lovington Atwood Hammond High School grad is headed to Lake Land Community College in Mattoon, Illinois, this fall to work toward an advanced degree in crop science.

Green's family business, Heritage Family Farms, specializes in corn and soybeans. A member of the FFA and a dedicated farmer, Green has been closely watching the tariff wars over the past few years. She says that she is passionate about agriculture and regularly "agvocates" for the future of farming in America.

Green has had to learn a lot about tariffs and trade to understand how these global economic negotiations are affecting her family's livelihood, and to speak out with an educated voice. "When China raises their tariffs, it costs more money to market a product to China and vice versa. In reality no one wants to pay that extra money, which in the end closes off the market," notes Green, who stresses that she agrees with President Trump's trade approach, but not his timing in an already-fragile agriculture economy.

"We export or sell a bunch of agriculture products to China. With their already high tariffs, and even higher tariffs after this trade war, there is a decreasing market to China," adds Green. "The problem is that American farmers are really good at what they do. We produce a surplus of products. This decreasing market coupled with a surplus of products means that the prices on our supply and demand-driven markets are not going to be good. Right now, the prices are so bad that many farmers are not even making their break-even prices, meaning they are losing money on their crops. Farmers are struggling. Big time. In the beginning the idea that we would get better prices and deals for our exported goods was something that many farmers in my area believed could be a good thing. At this point, though, farmers are losing hope."

Taking a "Hit Through It All"

Scott Ashby, 17 and a rising senior at Carroll Jr. Sr. High School in Carroll County, Indiana, is a third-generation family grain farmer. He says that the open land in places like Carroll County, which has 13 hogs to every two people, allows for a lot of farming diversity with crops as well as livestock. As a member of the FFA, Ashby believes he has a duty to inform people about the issues that affect farmers. "Almost everything in the world can be related back to agriculture," he says. "One decision can impact the entire world. You get a year like this with high rain values in Indiana and farmers have to push back planting. The next thing you know, not only does the nation but the entire world see higher prices due to the shortage of corn, soybeans and wheat that we failed to produce."

While the U.S.-China trade war impacts farming decisions that Ashby and his family make every day, he points out that their awareness of the global economic climate is a fundamental part of their job. "The U.S. farmer has been affected by the tariffs for a number of years through many different administrations, from things as simple as increased prices on over-the-counter parts at the dealership, due to shipping tariffs and importation costs, to reduced commodity prices. Farmers have taken a hit through it all," notes Ashby.

Surviving in the agriculture business means learning to adapt—and cuts costs, he adds. "We have responded to the trade war by holding our equipment over longer periods of time instead of trading up, along with doing more repairs ourselves or hiring outside mechanics not affiliated with a dealership to cut those costs," Ashby says. "We are also holding our grain for a longer period of time trying to wait it out for higher prices."

The U.S.-China trade war has spotlighted the struggles of farmers in the U.S., and both Green and Ashby want their generation to understand what hardships in agriculture mean for the country and the world. "Agriculture is the largest industry in Illinois and is one of the largest in the country. One in four people will go into a job related to agriculture," says Green, who was chosen as a national finalist last year in grain-production entrepreneurship. "Everyone needs a farmer every day all day for food, fiber and fuel. Without this industry, no one would eat, and the United States' economy would struggle. Times are tough now, and getting tougher. This is making coming back to the farm less and less attractive for young farmers. This is scary as the age of the U.S farmer is on the rise. We need farmers! We need family farms! They are the backbone of America and keep food on our tables and clothes on our backs. If we don't support farms and keep their doors open, it's hard to tell what will happen to the entire economy of the United States and the world."

Ashby echoes those sentiments, and adds that he believes in the foundation of farming as family businesses working and prospering through a connection with and appreciation for the land. "There will always be a future in agriculture; the only thing that concerns me is what that future looks like," says Ashby. "We already see big businesses infiltrating everything we do, from Monsanto buying out all of the competition across the globe, to companies such as Red Gold investing in their own ground and hiring farmers to tend to and produce a crop off of it, while [Red Gold] collects the main profits. There are also issues like mislabeling of consumer-related goods, such as General Mills saying that their wheat is non-GMO, while in fact wheat has never been genetically modified. Also, it is legal to label lab-grown meat as real meat, when by the Merriam-Webster dictionary, the term meat is defined as the flesh of an animal (particularly mammal) used as food. Ag may never look the same if we do not do our part to cure these myths and set the story straight about what agriculture truly is."

16

Fighting Food Insecurity

The New Humanitarian

The New Humanitarian is a news agency that focuses on humanitarian stories in regions that are often forgotten, under-reported, misunderstood, or ignored. Until 2015, the New Humanitarian was a project of the United Nations Office for the Coordination of Humanitarian Affairs.

The following viewpoint details efforts made and reported on in 2014 to boost food security in Afghanistan, a country struggling to grow enough food to feed its 31 million people. Through joint efforts with the UN World Food Programme and the Strategic Grain Reserve, the country aims to construct depots in various regions in the country that will hold 200,000 metric tons of food, which could potentially feed 2 million people for up to six months in times of emergency.

A network of critical emergency grain reserves across Afghanistan is set to boost food security and help strengthen resilience in a country that struggles to grow enough food to feed its 31 million people.

"Grain reserves for a country like Afghanistan are absolutely critical," Gerard Rebello, Head of Logistics & Pipeline at the UN World Food Programme (WFP), told IRIN. "Afghanistan is a landlocked country, so there needs to be a mechanism in place

"Fighting food insecurity in Afghanistan," The New Humanitarian, January 3, 2014. Reprinted by permission.

in case supplies cannot come in. The country's annual production does not meet the annual consumption, and it's a country that has recurrent natural disasters."

The first of a planned series of Strategic Grain Reserves (SGR), a warehouse with a 22,000 metric ton capacity, opened in late 2013 in the capital, Kabul, at a cost of US$7.7 million.

The WFP-Afghan government project aims to construct depots in various locations that will eventually hold a total of 200,000 metric tons of food—enough to feed two million people for up to six months in times of emergency. SGRs are planned for other cities, including Mazar-e-Sharif, Herat, Pul-i-Khumri and Kandahar.

"The 200,000 tons, which is the planned figure, is not a big amount," said Rebello. "But it is enough to buy time. It's enough to respond to small disasters while long-term help comes in."

Mujeed Qarar, a spokesman for the Ministry of Agriculture, Irrigation and Livestock (MAIL), pointed out that in recent years aid agencies have started shifting their focus to longer-term infrastructure projects. International troop numbers are being drawn down, and humanitarians fear donor funding is likely to diminish as attention turns elsewhere.

In 2009–10, reconstruction started on a separate existing network of long-term silos, which can store grain for up to two years.

Wheat Production

Wheat production in 2013 was the highest the country has experienced in the past 30 years, with the harvest estimated at around 6.5 million tons, according to MAIL.

Increased grain production is welcome, but food security is uneven, with poor transport links and distribution networks creating continuing challenges, not least in the winter months, when areas like Badakshan are cut off. Afghanistan is also prone to recurring drought and natural disasters.

National grain deficits are in the main filled by commercial imports from neighbouring Pakistan and Kazakhstan. But the global food price hikes of 2008 showed international markets cannot always be relied upon for freely available and affordable food. That year, wheat flour prices in Afghanistan doubled. The reserves should also bring greater stability to local grain markets.

Vulnerability

Internally displaced persons (IDPs) and returned Afghan refugees, who currently number around 536,000, are disproportionally exposed to food insecurity and malnutrition. According to UNICEF's 2013 mid-year report, the number of Afghans displaced by conflict increased by 7.4 percent from 2011 to 2012.

At the Indira Gandhi hospital in Kabul, a displaced 19-year-old mother, originally from Logar province in eastern Afghanistan, is seeking treatment for her child. "We cannot get my daughter enough food because my husband and other relatives are unemployed, and our harvest was not good this year because of the cold weather," she said. "We are not doing well economically, that is why she is suffering from malnutrition."

A report by the Famine Early Warning Systems Network (FEWS NET) in November 2013 raises concerns about increasing food security issues among IDPs, particularly those in western Herat province, bordering Iran.

Many families struggle during the winter months, when job opportunities are limited and the prices of necessities such as fuel, wood and oil are at their highest.

The head of the malnutrition ward at the Indira Gandhi hospital, Dr Saifullah Abasin, says up to 70 percent of the children in the hospital are underweight, and up to 85 percent are malnourished.

A 2012 World Bank report noted that on average, 29 percent of Afghans were not able to meet their daily requirement of 2,100 calories.

Children are particularly vulnerable. According to a WFP statement released in October 2013, 60 percent of children are facing malnutrition. "While security issues related to insurgency and foreign aggression monopolize most discourse in Afghanistan, a lesser noted form of insecurity—food and nutrition shortage—also threatens the country's prosperity," said the statement.

Challenges

A functioning Strategic Grain Reserve network will help provide resources to vulnerable populations, but rising insecurity poses a major challenge for humanitarians looking to provide food assistance.

"Security impacts us from a construction point of view, for example, access to supplies, and monitoring activities," said Keiko Izushi, WFP's Head of Donor Relations, Reports and Communications. "As of now, we don't see any complications, but if the situation becomes worse, these things could become more challenging."

A growing concern in the aid community is insecurity on roads, which are the principal means of transporting food. In the first eleven months of 2013, the UN Office for the Coordination of Humanitarian Affairs (OCHA) recorded 266 incidents against humanitarian personnel, facilities and assets.

Corruption Can Also Be a Challenge

"A major problem is that officials at the provincial level give distributions to their circle of people first, so rich and powerful people get food first and many times the people who need it, like farmers, do not receive anything," said an Afghan government official from Kunduz.

Emergency grain supplies have sometimes disappeared on their way to starving farmers in the north of the province. In other cases, government officials have been arrested while diverting food aid to local markets, and elsewhere leading officials have simply helped themselves to stored grain supplies.

"We are aware," said WFP's Izushi. "This is why we involve the government—it is part of our capacity building and training—but the state also has to take responsibility."

17

Support for Food Insecure Children

Kate Rosier

Kate Rosier is a research officer for the Australian Institute of Family Studies. She has recently published articles concerning empowerment evaluation and participatory action research for the Australian government.

In the following viewpoint, Kate Rosier details food insecurity through the specific lens of the children and families impacted in Australia. Rosier details the ways in which child and family services in the country can address the underlying factors that contribute to this specific case of food insecurity. The most impacted group in Australia is the indigenous population, including 30 percent of adults who have food security concerns due to poor income, household infrastructure, overcrowding, and access to transport, storage, and cooking facilities.

This practice sheet explores food insecurity in Australia with a focus on identifying those most likely to suffer it as well as considering its impacts.

Whilst often thought of in terms of third world countries, food insecurity is also prevalent in certain groups within wealthy countries like Australia. This practice sheet is designed to assist child and family services to address food insecurity amongst their clientele.

Key Messages

- There are three key components of food insecurity: inadequate access to food, inadequate supply and the inappropriate use of food (e.g., inappropriate preparation of food). The prevalence of food insecurity amongst the Australian population is estimated at 5%.
- Certain groups in Australia are more susceptible to food insecurity—including unemployed people, single parent households, low-income earners, rental households and young people.
- Indigenous, culturally and linguistically diverse (CALD) and socially isolated people may also experience food insecurity at a higher rate.
- The reasons why people experience food insecurity include: a lack of resources (including financial resources and other resources such as transport); lack of access to nutritious food at affordable prices, lack of access to food due to geographical isolation; and lack of motivation or knowledge about a nutritious diet.
- Food insecurity is a concern for child and family services organisations as it can impact negatively upon outcomes for children in the short and long-term—including children's academic ability and health issues including obesity, diabetes and heart disease.
- Child and family services in Australia can play a key role in improving the food security of their clients via a range of practical measures as well as referrals to services such as financial counselling that address underlying factors which may contribute to food insecurity.

What Is Food Insecurity?

Whereas food security is broadly defined as "access by all people at all times to enough food for an active, healthy life," food insecurity exists "whenever the availability of nutritionally adequate and safe foods or the ability to acquire acceptable food in socially acceptable ways is limited or uncertain." There are three key components of food security:

1. Food access: the capacity to acquire and consume a nutritious diet, including:

    - the ability to buy and transport food;
    - home storage, preparation and cooking facilities;
    - knowledge and skills to make appropriate choices;
    - and time and mobility to shop for and prepare food.

2. Food availability: the supply of food within a community affecting food security of individuals, households or an entire population, specifically:

    - location of food outlets;
    - availability of food within stores; and
    - price, quality and variety of available food.

3. Food use: the appropriate use of food based on knowledge of basic nutrition and care.

    There are three different "levels" of food security:

    - secure;
    - insecure but without hunger—where there may be anxiety or uncertainty about access to food or inappropriate use of food (i.e., poor nutritional quality) but regular consumption of food occurs; and
    - insecure with extreme hunger—where meals are often missed or inadequate.

According to the United Nations World Food Summit in 1996, food security is a right for all people. Yet conservative estimates suggest that upwards of 5% of Australians experience food insecurity, 40% of those at a severe level.

Who Experiences Food Insecurity in Australia and Why?

According to the 1995 Australian National Nutrition Survey and the Aboriginal and Torres Strait Islander Health Performance Framework (data 2004-05) certain groups experience food insecurity at a higher rate than the general population. These groups include:

- Indigenous people (24%);
- unemployed people (23%);
- single parent households (23%);
- low-income earners (20%);
- rental households (20%); and
- young people (15%).

Other people who are susceptible to food insecurity include:

- some culturally and linguistically diverse (CALD) groups including refugees;
- people who do not have access to private and/or public transport;
- people who misuse alcohol and tobacco; and
- people who are disabled, unwell or frail.

The reasons why some of these groups experience food insecurity are outlined below.

Indigenous Populations

Indigenous populations may be vulnerable to food insecurity, with 30% of Indigenous adults reporting being worried about going without food. Rates of food insecurity are highest in remote communities. However, Indigenous people living in urban environments are also vulnerable to food insecurity due to poor income, household infrastructure and overcrowding, access to transport, storage and cooking facilities.

In remote locations, food supply is often limited to a "general store" that is not always open, and is often expensive, with a 26% higher price of a "basket of food" in remote community stores when compared with a Darwin supermarket.

Coupled with the high percentage of residents in remote communities earning a low income, Indigenous people must spend a greater percentage of their income on meals than non-Indigenous Australians—at least 35% according to Northern Territory Government statistics. Much of this is spent on ready-made meals from fast food outlets that may vary in nutritional quality. However they are often more convenient as these outlets may be open longer hours than the general store.

Furthermore, other resources may be limited in remote communities—such as a working stove or oven. One survey of almost four thousand Indigenous homes in the Northern Territory found that only 38% had facilities such as stoves, ovens, running water and adequate storage for food. This further encourages a reliance on ready made, and often nutritionally poor foods.

CALD Groups

Some CALD groups have also been found to experience food insecurity due to a departure from their traditional diets when relocating to Australia, with a failure to take up nutritious alternatives. People who have recently relocated to Australia may lack nutritional education about food available in their local supermarket, which may vary dramatically from what was available in their country of origin.

Low-Income Families

Economic barriers to food security are common and low-income families often experience challenges in purchasing adequate quantities of food, as well as appropriately healthy food. Concerns about the higher costs of food sometimes experienced by low income families and people living in remote areas (especially Indigenous remote communities) mean that food insecurity is high amongst low-income people and families.

Middle income families who have recently had a drop in income (i.e., through job loss) or who have high living expenses may also experience food insecurity due to a lack of available funds to allocate to food purchases.

Lack of Access to Private and/or Public Transport

Other barriers such as lack of car ownership in high population areas and/or poorly organised public transport to retail centres may confine disadvantaged people to buying food locally where there may be less choice and higher prices. Geographical isolation may also contribute to food insecurity, possibly along with inadequate transport. Remote areas may have fewer large supermarkets forcing residents to be dependent on smaller shops which stock a limited range of foods, sometimes of lower quality, and often, higher prices.

People Suffering Illness, Frailness, or Other Forms of Social Isolation

People suffering illness, frailness or other forms of social isolation may also experience food insecurity regardless of their financial means, due to an inability to either purchase or prepare adequate food as a result of their condition. Similarly, people with substance abuse conditions may not purchase or prepare adequate food for themselves or their families, either because their material resources are spent on drugs or alcohol, or simply because they are not functioning adequately to attend to these tasks.

Why Is Food Security an Important Issue for Child and Family Services?

The prevalence of food insecurity amongst the Australian population (a conservative estimate of 5%) suggests that child and family services are likely to encounter families that are experiencing this problem. Many child and family services will be supporting children and families who fit one or more of the characteristics that make them more vulnerable to food insecurity (e.g., unemployed, single parent households and living in rented accommodation) and, as such, these services are more likely to encounter clients who experience food insecurity.

In Australia, food security is considered to be an important social determinant of health and a significant public health issue at national and state levels. Food insecurity is, however, especially important to child and family services because of the negative impact food security can have on parents and children, both in the short and long term.

For example, food security has been shown to affect academic achievement in children, both in ability upon commencement at school, and in learning over the school year. Food insecurity is especially relevant to the current "obesity epidemic" amongst Australian children as Australian data indicate that the risk of obesity is higher in those who experience (mild to moderate) food insecurity. While this might seem illogical, it is due to the tendency of food insecure people to purchase cheaper food, which is often much lower in nutritional content and higher in fat, salt and sugar content and refined carbohydrates (starch).

Food insecurity is also associated with general poor health, and may worsen other health inequalities that are apparent in disadvantaged groups such as a higher mortality rate, and higher rates of coronary heart disease, type-2 diabetes and some cancers. Furthermore, poor nutrition is associated with low birth weight and ill health in infancy and childhood.

Nutritional Challenges

The nutritional aspect of food security is often overlooked in favor of simply ensuring people are eating regular meals. However, an important part of food security is access to "nutritionally adequate and safe foods." Public health recommendations for an adult to eat five serves each of breads/cereals and vegetables, as well as two serves of fruit per day are often not feasible for those who are welfare dependent or earning a low income. International studies report that healthy food is more expensive than unhealthy food, and local studies have shown that people in welfare or low-income categories are less likely to buy and eat healthy food.

In their study into the costs of a healthy diet, Kettings et al. found that welfare dependent families needed to spend at least 33% of their weekly income to eat according to public health recommendations if they bought generic brands. For families earning an "average" wage, 25% of the income of a single parent household and 18% of a dual parent household was required to meet these eating guidelines. They concluded that at a cost of 33% of the household income, healthy food habits are economically challenging for welfare dependent families.

An important aspect of food security for families is breastfeeding. Breastfeeding can be an effective method of reducing food insecurity for infants especially for disadvantaged families who may not be able to afford sufficient amounts of infant formula to adequately meet infant dietary needs. Australia's dietary guidelines recommend that infants are breastfed until 6 months of age.

One of the many ways of addressing food insecurity is via the distribution of "food parcels" through community service agencies. However, anecdotal reports are that these parcels tend to be stocked with non-perishable goods, due to the storage capabilities of the agencies involved. (Food banks—organisations that receive donations of food and have large storage capabilities—may be able to supply community service agencies with fresh foods on a regular basis. Aboriginal community, see Early Learnings Telstra Foundation Research Report.) As a result, those families receiving food parcels miss out on fresh food, which can be helpful in maintaining a balanced diet that meets recommended dietary guidelines. It is important to note, however, that food parcels can free up some of the food budget, which may be then directed to purchasing fresh goods.

Also, as there is increasing pressure on the community services sector to respond to growing disadvantage, agencies and workers may need additional support, such as additional resources and training to ensure that clients' nutritional requirements are met.

Practice Considerations

These practice considerations are general principles based upon lessons from research and practice designed to provide additional guidance to service providers about working with individuals and families experiencing food insecurity.

How Can Services Support Families Experiencing Food Insecurity?

Measures to address food security include short, medium or long-term solutions. Some services can directly assist families in the short-term by providing food parcels, food vouchers and/or meals. Most services will have some information available about local services that can provide these services.

As many services will already be providing short-term support, the following practice considerations focus upon medium and long-term measures for supporting families who experience food insecurity. Policy measures are also considered.

Education

- Nutritional education is often poor amongst disadvantaged populations and as such whilst the quantity of food supplies may be adequate in these households, their quality may be poor and fail to meet the nutritional needs of family members, particularly children.
- Nutritional education in languages other than English may be necessary for some CALD groups.
- Simple techniques like planning meals in advance and writing a shopping list with only required ingredients help to keep food costs lower and ensure value for money. Planning meals ahead also helps to reduce dependency on expensive and often unhealthy take-away meals.

- Lack of familiarity with food preparation and/or ingredients may be a deterrent to the preparation of fresh healthy meals. Basic food preparation techniques and a guided shopping exercise can help to reduce these barriers and improve knowledge and confidence in food preparation.
- A familiarity of public health recommendations for healthy eating is essential for staff dealing with food insecure clients. It may also be useful to educate clients and help them to implement these recommendations through suggested meal plans or other practical examples.

Questions to Consider

- Are there any services in the local community that can provide parents with food budgeting advice and/or offer food purchasing and preparation classes? In some localities, community kitchens these types of educational opportunities along with facilities to communally prepare and share meals.
- If your service provides food parcels or meals directly to clients, are staff confident about their knowledge of nutrition? Could professional development opportunities involve nutritional education?
- Are clients provided with information about healthy eating? Is this information presented in a way that is accessible to clients (e.g., plain English)? Is information available in languages other than English?

Resources

- Families who do not have access to private and/or public transport can have difficulties getting their grocery shopping home. Another barrier for some families is a lack of adequate refrigeration. Both these factors can also impede a family's ability to purchase or maintain the quality of fresh food.

- Buying groceries in bulk is a good way to save money on goods, however this can often be difficult for low-income families who lack the initial funds to outlay on bulk purchases. Lack of access to transport and lack of adequate refrigeration can further restrict a family's ability to purchase food in bulk.

Questions to Consider

- Is it possible for your service to subsidise the home delivery of groceries for clients who have difficulties with transport? Is there another service in the community that can provide clients with this support? Do you know of supermarkets or other shops in the local area that provide free home delivery for customers?
- Can your service assist clients to obtain refrigeration appliances? Is there another service in the community that can provide clients with this support?
- Community kitchens could organise "buy in bulk" services for multiple families. This allows families to share the cost of buying in bulk. Is there are a community kitchen in the local community that provides this type of service?

Information and Referral

A range of services and resources in the local community can be useful to families experiencing food insecurity. Providing information and/or referral to these services can help these families. These resources may include:

- *community gardens:* plots of land set aside within a community where community members may grow plants and/or vegetables and fruit. Community garden projects can be a cost effective and enjoyable way for clients and their families to acquire fresh food;
- *school "breakfast clubs":* offer morning meals to students whose families may be financially disadvantaged or suffer another form of food insecurity;
- *financial counselling or other services:* may help to address long term issues which play a major role in food insecurity; and

- *lists of local markets or lower cost retail options for food purchasing:* may help clients to get better value out of their food budget.

Questions to Consider

- Are there community gardens, breakfast clubs or other appropriate services or resources within the local community? If so, are clients provided with information about these services and resources?

Policy Measures

It is important to consider policy measures that may impact on food security. Service providers can advocate locally for policies that may improve food security in their geographical area such as policies that:

- encourage food manufacturers and wholesalers to dispose of surplus food through food banks—via economic incentives or other means;
- reflect the higher cost of food in remote areas;
- address provision for special needs diets;
- aim to improve nutritional standards and knowledge within the community (i.e., public health policies); and
- support local production of food and improved transport to food outlets.

What Do Food Security Programs Look Like in Practice?

There are a range of programs and projects in Australia that address the issue of food security. CAFCA's Promising Practice Profiles database provides some examples of these types of programs and projects.

One example is a community kitchen pilot project based in Frankston, Victoria. This program aims to improve participants' food security through acquiring food knowledge and skills whilst reducing social isolation. The issues it seeks to address are food access and use: the poor physical and financial access to quality, affordable fresh produce, which in turn is a barrier to healthy eating for some community members. A variety of community members—including aged, Indigenous, disadvantaged, youth and migrant individuals—make use of the community kitchen facilities.

Using a flexible and negotiable approach, the project requires active participation and financial contribution from group members. It does not sell food but rather educates participants in the planning and cooking of meals. Training workshops are provided for facilitators and interested participants, covering topics such as healthy eating, budgeting for food, kitchen and food safety and group facilitation. All other education for participants is informal and involves the ongoing weekly gathering of 6-8 people and one facilitator who jointly select and prepare meals that they then share together for a small investment of a few dollars.

Notable outcomes of the program include:

- improvements in cooking skills, nutritional knowledge, meal planning, budgeting and shopping habits;
- increased fruit and vegetable consumption (43%) and reduction of fast food consumption (64%);
- improvements in food safety and hygiene practices;
- significant impacts on participants mental health and wellbeing due to the social aspect of the project (social inclusion); and
- an increase in community strength, with 43% of participants going on to join other community groups.

Organizations to Contact

The editors have compiled the following list of organizations concerned with the issues debated in this book. The descriptions are derived from materials provided by the organizations. All have publications or information available for interested readers. The list was compiled on the date of publication of the present volume; the information provided here may change. Be aware that many organizations take several weeks or longer to respond to inquiries, so allow as much time as possible.

Agriculture and Agri-Food Canada
1341 Baseline Road
Ottawa, ON K1A 0C5
phone: (855) 773-0241
email: aafc.info.aac@canada.ca
website: www.agr.gc.ca

The Agriculture and Agri-Food Canada Department of the Canadian government works with farmers and food producers to support the growth and development of the agriculture and agri-food sector. Their policies, programs, research, and technology help them succeed in Canadian and global markets. Agriculture is also a shared jurisdiction in Canada, and the department works closely with provincial and territorial governments in the development and delivery of policies and programs.

Asia Pacific Foundation of Canada (APF Canada)
900-675 W. Hastings Street
Vancouver, BC V6B 1N2
Canada
phone: (604) 684-5986
email: info@asiapacific.ca
website: www.asiapacific.ca

The Asia Pacific Foundation of Canada (APF Canada) is a nonprofit organization focused on Canada's relations with Asia. APF Canada is dedicated to strengthening ties between Canada and Asia with a focus on expanding economic relations through trade, investment, and innovation, and creating solutions to issues like climate change, energy, food security, and natural resource management challenges.

The Faculty of Public Health (FPH)
4 St. Andrews Place
London, NW1 4LB
United Kingdom
phone: 020 3696 1463
email: alineoshima@fph.org.uk
website: www.fph.org.uk

The Faculty of Public Health (FPH) is a membership organization for nearly 4,000 public health professionals across the UK and around the world. They are also a registered charity. Their role is to improve the health and wellbeing of local communities and national populations.

The Food and Agriculture Organization of the United Nations (FAO)
Viale delle Terme di Caracalla
00153 Rome
Italy
phone: (+39) 06 57051
email: FAO-HQ@fao.org
website: www.fao.org

The Food and Agriculture Organization (FAO) is a specialized agency of the United Nations that leads international efforts to defeat hunger. Their goal is to achieve food security for all and make sure that people have regular access to enough high-quality food to lead active, healthy lives. With over 194 member states, FAO works in over 130 countries worldwide. They believe that everyone can play a part in ending hunger.

Food Empowerment Project

PO Box 7322
Cotati, CA 94931
phone: (707) 779-8004
email: info@foodispower.org
website: www.foodispower.org

The Food Empowerment Project seeks to create a more just and sustainable world by recognizing the power of one's food choices. They encourage healthy food choices that reflect a more compassionate society by spotlighting the abuse of animals on farms, the depletion of natural resources, unfair working conditions for produce workers, and the unavailability of healthy foods in low-income areas. They also work to discourage negligent corporations from pushing unhealthy foods into low-income areas and empower people to make healthier choices by growing their own fruits and vegetables. In all of their work, Food Empowerment Project seeks specifically to empower those with the fewest resources.

Mercy Corps

PO Box 80020
Prescott, AZ 86304-9801
phone: 1 (888) 842-0842
email: lhector@mercycorps.org
website: www.mercycorps.org

Through close collaboration with community members and a wide variety of organizations, Mercy Corps puts bold solutions into action and helps people triumph over adversity. The organization aims to connect people to the resources they need to build better, stronger lives.

The United Nations Children's Fund (UNICEF)

125 Maiden Lane, 11th Floor
New York, NY 10038
phone: (212) 686-5522
website: www.unicef.org

UNICEF promotes the rights and wellbeing of every child. They work in 190 countries and territories to translate that commitment into practical action, focusing special effort on reaching the most vulnerable and excluded children, to the benefit of all children. In all of its work, UNICEF takes a life-cycle based approach, recognizing the particular importance of early childhood development and adolescence. UNICEF programs focus on the most disadvantaged children, including those living in fragile contexts, those with disabilities, those who are affected by rapid urbanization, and those affected by environmental degradation.

United States Department of Agriculture (USDA)
1400 Independence Avenue SW
Washington, DC 20250
phone: (202) 401-7211
email: feedback@usda.gov
website: www.usda.gov

The USDA provides leadership on food, agriculture, natural resources, rural development, nutrition, and related issues based on public policy, the best available science, and effective management. They have a vision to provide economic opportunity through innovation, helping rural America to thrive; to promote agriculture production that better nourishes Americans while also helping feed others throughout the world; and to preserve the nation's natural resources through conservation, restored forests, improved watersheds, and healthy private working lands.

Bibliography

Books

Howard G. Buffett and Howard W. Buffett. *40 Chances: Finding Hope in a Hungry World*. New York, NY: Simon & Schuster, 2014.

Harriet Dyer. *The Little Book of Going Green: Really Understand Climate Change, Use Greener Products, Adopt a Tree, Save Water, and Much More!* New York, NY: Skyhorse Publishing, 2019.

Jenny Eaton Dyer and Cathleen Falsani. *The End of Hunger: Renewed Hope for Feeding the World*. Westmont, IL: IVP Books, 2019.

Jeremy K. Everett. *I Was Hungry: Cultivating Common Ground to End an American Crisis*. Ada, MI: Brazos Press, 2019.

Andrew Fisher. *Big Hunger: The Unholy Alliance between Corporate America and Anti-Hunger Groups (Food, Health, and the Environment)*. Cambridge, MA: MIT Press, 2017.

Duncan Green. *How Change Happens*. Oxford, UK: Oxford University Press, 2016.

J. Harrigan. *The Political Economy of Arab Food Sovereignty*. London, UK: Palgrave Macmillan, 2014.

Frances Moore Lappe and Joseph Collins. *World Hunger*. New York, NY: Grove Atlantic, 2015.

Howard D. Leathers and Phillips Foster. *The World Food Problem, 5th ed.: Toward Understanding and Ending Undernutrition in the Developing World*. Bounder, CO: Lynne Reinner Publishers, 2017.

Paul McMahon. *Feeding Frenzy: Land Grabs, Price Spikes, and the World Food Crisis*. Vancouver, BC: Greystone Books, 2014.

Tracie McMillan. *The American Way of Eating: Undercover at Walmart, Applebee's, Farm Fields and the Dinner Table.* New York, NY: Scribner, 2012.

Kristin D. Phillips. *An Ethnography of Hunger: Politics, Subsistence, and the Unpredictable Grace of the Sun.* Bloomington, IN: Indiana University Press, 2018.

Peter Pringle. *A Place at the Table: The Crisis of 49 Million Hungry Americans and How to Solve It.* New York, NY: Public Affairs, 2013.

Jeremy Rifkin. *The Green New Deal: Why the Fossil Fuel Civilization Will Collapse by 2028, and the Bold Economic Plan to Save Life on Earth.* New York, NY: St. Martin's Press, 2019.

Ute Scheub, Haiko Pieplow, Hans-Peter Schmidt, et al. *Terra Preta: How the World's Most Fertile Soil Can Help Reverse Climate Change and Reduce World Hunger.* Vancouver, BC: Greystone Books, 2016.

C. Peter Timmer. *Food Security and Scarcity: Why Ending Hunger Is So Hard.* Philadelphia, PA: University of Pennsylvania Press, 2015.

Periodicals and Internet Sources

Jane Battersby and Jonathan Crush, "Africa's Urban Food Deserts," *Urban Forum*, 2014, https://link.springer.com/article/10.1007/s12132-014-9225-5.

Jason Beaubien, "The Fight Against World Hunger Is Going in the Wrong Direction," NPR, September 11, 2018, https://www.npr.org/sections/goatsandsoda/2018/09/11/646786468/the-fight-against-world-hunger-is-going-in-the-wrong-direction.

Jessica Booth, "Everything You Need to Know About Food Deserts," *Redbook*, April 29, 2019, https://www

.redbookmag.com/food-recipes/a27288617/food-deserts
-in-america/.

Sarah Bosley, "World hunger on the rise as 820m at risk, UN report finds," *Guardian*, July 15, 2019, https://www .theguardian.com/world/2019/jul/15/world-hunger-un -report.

Anna Brones, "Food apartheid: the root of the problem with America's groceries," *Guardian*, May 15, 2018, https://www .theguardian.com/society/2018/may/15/food-apartheid -food-deserts-racism-inequality-america-karen -washington-interview.

Anna Casano, "Here Are All of the US's Largest Food Deserts," *Ranker*, 2018, https://www.ranker.com/list/largest-food -deserts-in-united-states/anncasano.

Jason Daley, "World Hunger Is on the Rise for the Third Year in a Row," *Smithsonian Magazine,* September 13, 2018. https:// www.smithsonianmag.com/smart-news/world-hunger-rise -third-year-row-180970281/.

Christopher Flavelle, "Climate Change Threatens the World's Food Supply, United Nations Warns," *New York Times,* August 8, 2019, https://www.nytimes.com/2019/08/08 /climate/climate-change-food-supply.html.

Jason Hickel, "The Global Food Crisis Is Here," *Foreign Policy,* August 21, 2019, https://foreignpolicy.com/2019/08/21/the -global-food-crisis-is-here/.

Joseph Hincks, "The World Is Headed for a Food Security Crisis. Here's How We Can Avert It," *Time*, March 28, 2018, https://time.com/5216532/global-food-security-richard -deverell/.

"An introduction to the basic concepts of food security," Food and Agriculture Organization, 2008, http://www.fao.org /docrep/013/al936e/al936e00.pdf.

Smitha Mundasad, "Global hunger increasing, UN warn," BBC, September 11, 2018, https://www.bbc.com/news /health-45477930.

Katie Pyzyk, "Mitigating America's food desert dilemma," Smartcities Dive, May 7, 2019, https://www.smartcitiesdive .com/news/mitigating-americas-food-desert-dilemma /554087/.

"The Top 10 Causes of World Hunger," Concern Worldwide US, May 27, 2019, https://concernusa.org/story/top-causes -world-hunger/.

"2019 World Hunger and Poverty Facts and Statistics," *Hunger Notes,* World Hunger Education Service, May 25, 2018, https://www.worldhunger.org/world-hunger-and-poverty -facts-and-statistics/.

Sarah Whitley, "Changing Times in Rural America: Food Assistance and Food Insecurity in Food Deserts," *Journal of Family Social Work*, February 5, 2013, https://www .tandfonline.com/doi/abs/10.1080/10522158.2012.736080.

"World Hunger: Facts & how to help," World Vision, October 25, 2019, https://www.worldvision.ca/stories/food/world -hunger-facts-how-to-help.

Index